Historian Wylie says:

"Amid the mountains of the Alps was an ancient church, resting on the foundations of Scripture, and protesting against the idolatrous corruptions of Rome."

"History of Protestantism," b. 3, ch. 19.

CHAMPIONS OF CHRISTIANITY

IN SEARCH OF TRUTH

VOLUME 1
in the series
GENUINE CHRISTIANITY

By
Ronald Charles Thompson

TEACH Services, Inc.
Brushton, New York

The author assumes full responsibility for the accuracy of all facts and quotations as cited in this book.

ISBN 1-57258-122-0
Library of Congress Catalog Card No. 96-61083

Published by

TEACH Services, Inc.
RR 1, Box 182
Brushton, New York 12916

**DEDICATED
TO
LAYMEN, SEMINARIANS
AND THEOLOGIANS
OF
PROTESTANTISM**

To Commemorate Luther's contribution
to Christianity on the occasion
of the
450th ANNIVERSARY
of Martin Luther's death.

TABLE OF CONTENTS

PHOTOS AND ILLUSTRATIONS viii

FOREWORD ix

PROLOGUE xi

INTRODUCTION 1

A GUIDED TOUR IN SEARCH OF TRUTH (PART 1) 7

A GUIDED TOUR IN SEARCH OF TRUTH (PART 2) 24

RISE OF THE CHURCH AT ROME 38

RISE OF THE CHURCH IN THE WILDERNESS 54

THE PROTESTANT REFORMATION 74

THE COUNTER REFORMATION 86

THE RADICAL REFORMATION 94

THE GREAT REVIVAL 109

LAST DAY CHURCH AND THE TESTIMONY OF JESUS 116

APPENDICES 145

BIBLIOGRAPHY 149

PHOTOS AND ILLUSTRATIONS

Photos

1 Statue of Saint Peter 9
2 "Thou art Peter" 10
3 Altar of the Chair, St. Peter's 12
4 Reformation Monument, Geneva, Switzerland 21
4a Monument Exploded View 21
5 Luther Memorial, Worms, Germany 22
5a Pre-Reformation quartet 22
5b Peter Waldo 22
6 Daniel's Quartet of Apocalyptical Beasts, Town Hall, Nuremberg, Germany 28
6a Four-headed Leopard & Ten-horned Beast 28
6b Little Horn 28
7 Huguenot Monument, Fransch Hoek, Cape, South Africa 34
8 Arch of Constantine, Rome, Italy 39
9 Waldensian Monument, Angrogna Valley, Cottian Alps, Italy 71
9a Monument Motto 71

Illustrations

1. The Metallic Statue of Daniel, Chapter Two 18
2. Comparison of Prophecies of Daniel 2 and Daniel 7 26
3. The Waldensian movement in the Middle Ages 65
4. Deflection of Antichrist either Backward or Forward 90

FOREWORD
A HUMAN INTEREST GLIMPSE OF THE AUTHOR AND HIS BOOK

Ronald Thompson, of British descent, was born and raised in Zimbabwe, Africa. While attending school in the British tradition, he developed an affinity for the subject of history. At the age of eleven years he won a prize in a national essay competition. He wrote a sixteen page history of the early British occupation of Zimbabwe.

At that early age, Ronald was not aware that God might have given him a spiritual gift for history. In later years he earned the Master's degree in secular history. He went on to graduate from the prestigious Rhodes University, Grahamstown, South Africa; that had a Chair of Divinity endowed by the Anglican, Congregational, Methodist, and Presbyterian churches of South Africa. Ronald was the only one that year, 1979, to receive from the Faculty of Divinity, the degree of Doctor of Philosophy in Ecclesiastical History.

A comical turn of events took place, while Ronald was doing undergraduate work in pursuit of Arts and Theology. It happened in his third year while studying a course on the Protestant Reformation. Apparently he had given a fiery sermonette in the auditorium. A fellow student immediately posted a 'bull' of condemnation, a facsimile of the one against Luther. It read "*Exsurge Domine...Ronaldo Tompono*"....

Ronaldo Tompono withdrew the posted "bull" and proceeded to the court yard at evening. In the presence of fellow students he ceremonially burned the bull. Reaction set in. A group of students immediately grabbed him, and carried his supine body down to the frog-pond swimming pool for a ducking. The ducking might have been quite refreshing, but the Dean of the Men's Residence, Professor Sparrow, thought there was a student uprising, and like a bird he "flew" into the scene, and called off the prank.

I don't know if Ronald was out for Reform, back in his student days. But he certainly took a shine to Martin Luther. And his book, "Champions of Christianity, In Search of Truth," revolves around Luther more than any other Champion, because it is written to commemorate the four hundred and fiftieth anniversary of the death of Luther.

The author dedicates his book to Protestantism, after a mature gospel ministry exceeding three decades, as a missionary to Uganda, and gospel minister and evangelist in Southern Africa and the United States. Specializing in the field of ecclesiastical history and historical theology, his book gives evidence of sound historical scholarship and penetrating insight, combined with extensive travel.

Following in the footsteps of Luther, Ron Thompson pulls no punches in setting forth the truths of Scripture, arguing from the base of the Scriptures alone—*sola scriptura*. Such is his battle-cry, from a book that is saturated with Scripture.

Following in the footsteps of Luther, Dr. Ron Thompson wants to finish the Reformation that was started by Luther. His book will tell you how this may be achieved. What an exciting challenge to Protestantism! Read all about it from the Introduction to the Epilogue.

Pieter E. Barkhuizen, Th.D.

PROLOGUE
INITIAL APPEAL TO PROTESTANTISM

Christian and Courteous Reader:

The grand theme and scope of this book burst into bloom, November 21, 1992. Before the inspiration faded, I immediately committed my pen to paper to record the initial general outline. This was the culmination of thoughts that were brewing since 1969. But, concerted research and note-taking only began after the outline was written.

I took to the writing of the book in mid-1995, like a "duck to water." Since there were times that I found myself in "deep waters" about what to write, and knew that I would either have to "sink or swim," I needed someone to rescue me from "sinking." The rescue was in God—*en theos*. I needed an infusion of *en theos*: en-thusiasm, Godly enthusiasm, to be possessed, or impressed by God. So, I dropped to my knees and prayed for freedom of expression and elucidation of truth. Several times in this posture clarity of thought and theme seized my mind. I acknowledge, and am thankful for the direction and leading of the Lord in writing this book.

The purview of this book is immense—it covers nearly fifteen hundred years, from the Constantinian era to the Wesleyan era. It is the Drama of the Ages, tracing the hand of God in the history of Redemption, and man's search for truth. Many tears of compassion have been shed in writing about those who "were slain for the Word of God, and for the testimony which they held" (Revelation 6:9). On the other hand, I have wept tears of joy while writing about those who have responded to the Word of God and the Testimony of Jesus (Revelation 1:2; 12:17).

This book has been written with a pen dipped in love. I have written without prejudice or rancor against any communion, church, or ecclesiastical movement. Any judgments made are based on a plain, "Thus saith the Lord," my only appeal is the truth from the Scriptures alone—*sola scriptura*. If there is any finger-pointing, it is derived from the facts of history, and the prophecies of Holy Scripture—which I am dependent upon.

In this year 1996, the four hundred and fiftieth year after the death of Dr. Martin Luther, I want to commemorate his great contribution to Christianity, in launching the Protestant Reformation. My Appeal to modern Protestantism, on this auspicious 450th anniversary of Luther's death, is to CONSIDER YOUR ROOTS. Recall how Protestantism arose in the first place.

When Protestants consider their roots, they will be amazed how it began. Was it ordained of God? Why did Protestantism arise? On what grounds did it take place? Was it just an inevitable event of history? Did it have its origin in Scripture?

It is the purpose of this book to remind Protestantism that it arose from the discovery of great Scriptural Truths. But, it is unfortunate that these truths were eventually *lost* to Protestantism, or they were bypassed. The loss of these truths are tantamount, then, to a denial of the Divine Origin of Protestantism.

The purpose of this book will be to *recover* these lost truths, to explain them in full, and to restore them fully. "Champions of Christianity in Search of Truth," will show when and where these monumental truths were discovered, and how they launched the greatest upheaval of Christianity—the Protestant Reformation. Phenomenal statements from ancient documents, that have been lost sight of, will reveal Biblical truths. Some of the greatest cover-ups of history will be revealed in this book, *the greatest Search for Truth ever published.*

Against a background of history and prophecy,
this book depicts two churches: one church (Revelation 17)
as a DEPARTURE FROM CHRIST,
the other as a church (Revelation 12) DRAWN TO CHRIST.

INTRODUCTION
THE SEARCH FOR TRUTH

From the beginning Eve did not believe God, who forbade eating fruit from the tree of knowledge of good and evil with the warning, "in the day thou eatest thereof, thou shalt surely die" (Genesis 2:17). Instead, Eve believed the devil who said, "Ye shall not surely die" (Genesis 3:4), and she went ahead and ate the forbidden fruit. Thus, Adam and Eve believed the lie of the devil and passed on a legacy to mankind who is prone to believe a lie rather than the truth.

Before the devil perpetrated his lie he insinuated doubt in the mind of Eve by the statement, "Yea, hath God said, Ye shall not eat of every tree of the garden?" (Genesis 3:1). Thus, the legacy of doubt and unbelief was passed on to the posterity of Adam. "For as by one man's disobedience many were made sinners, so by the obedience of one shall many be made righteous" (Romans 5:19).

The departure from truth experienced by Adam and Eve we would label: The Great Fall. Next, in succession to fall was Cain, who instead of presenting a lamb for sacrifice, to express faith in the blood of the Lamb of God as the promised atonement, brought the first-fruits of the earth as a thank offering. There was no efficacy in what he offered, for, "without shedding of blood is no remission" (Hebrews 9:22).

Abel, on the other hand, did not depend upon his own efforts like Cain did, for salvation, neither did he render partial obedience. True faith, as exercised by Abel, relies wholly upon Christ and is manifested in obedience to all the requirements and truths of God. It is no wonder then, that Abel's name was inscribed on the honor roll of faith: "By faith Abel offered unto God a more excellent sacrifice than Cain, by which he obtained witness that he was righteous" (Hebrews 11:4). Cain continued to fall away and pursue an unrighteous life when he murdered his brother Abel, "because his own works were evil, and his brother's righteous" (1 John 3:12).

Further down through time Israel followed the trends of Adam and Eve and Cain, as outlined above, but at other times Israel revived and reformed, and were faithful to the truths of God. In other words the history of Israel was one of Apostasy and Reform.

While it is readily accepted that Israel slipped into apostasy and out into renewal from time to time, it is not generally accepted nowadays, that spiritual Israel, namely the Christian Church, could also fall away and have need for renewal, revival and reformation.

It is the purpose of this book to trace the Apostasy or Great Fall Away of the Church "because they received not the love of the truth, that they might be saved. And for this cause God shall send them strong delusion, that they should believe a lie" (2 Thessalonians 2:10,11).

The Historic Apostasy of the Church will be traced as a "departure from Christ," while on the other hand the true church will be traced, which was motivated by the "testimony of Jesus" (Revelation 1:2), because the "truth is in Jesus" (Ephesians 4:21), who emphatically declared, "I am the way, the truth, and the life" (John 14:6).

Jesus declared: "And I, if I be lifted upon from the earth, will draw all men unto me" (John 12:32). In contrast to the church that was a "departure from Christ," will be traced the history of the church that was "drawn to Christ." This story of the true church has scarcely been told in full, as Champions of Christianity in Search of Truth recover and restore lost truths and discover new truths. What a thrilling experience you are going to have as you read the following pages and discover truths you did not know.

HOW TO SEARCH FOR TRUTH IN SCRIPTURE

Of course all the truths you'll come across in this treatise are in your Bible anyway, if you'll just search for them. "Search the Scriptures; for in them ye think ye have eternal life: and they are they which testify of me" (John 5:39).

We must understand that "All scripture is given by inspiration of God, and is profitable for doctrine, for reproof, for correction, for instruction in righteousness: that the man of God may be perfect" (2 Timothy 3:16). Notice "all scripture" means the entire Bible—Old and New Testament. That means no selection of certain portions, to the exclusion of others, just to satisfy our curiosity, or to satisfy our likes and dislikes, or what we would like to follow and obey.

While the Bible writers were inspired by God and "holy men of God spake as they were moved by the Holy Ghost" (2 Peter 1:19), they wrote their own words with all their human frailties and inadequacies—they were not all literary giants. The words are not inspired, but the thoughts are. Bible writers were oblivious to the present day rules of introduction—body—conclusion. Some writers just rambled on, often repeating themselves, not always reasoning from cause to effect, but the reverse. Sequence of events, chronology, development of thought in paragraph form, and transition from one thought to another was not always uppermost in their writing skill.

Simple Rule for Bible Study

Then we come along with our twentieth century training and are inclined to read our literary forms and rules of expression into the Scriptures. Instead, take the Scriptures at face value, *prima facie*, arriving at the literal, common sense, of what is written, a plain, "Thus saith the Lord." Realize that when a passage says one thing, it does not mean another. Any translation of ancient language demands concentration on the passage to be understood. Even the apostle Peter acknowledged that Paul's epistles in the original language had "some things hard to be understood" (2 Peter 3:16).

So, how is one able to arrive at truth in searching the Scriptures? Since present day Bibles are written in verse form making up a chapter, it is very easy for one to slip into the error of interpreting a verse or text of Scripture out of context. Read the whole chapter. And if that does not arrive at truth, read more from that particular book of the Bible. Further light may be obtained by reading other Biblical books by the same author, and thereafter read other contemporary Biblical books by other authors on the same subject. Marginal, or central reference columns in the Bible, aid the reader in giving other Scriptural passages pertinent to the subject. In this approach to the Word of God one is following the Bible injunction of comparing Scripture with Scripture. "Whom shall He teach knowledge and whom shall he make to understand doctrine? For precept must be upon precept, precept upon precept; line upon line, line upon line, here a little, and there a little" (Isaiah 28:9,10).

7 Rules for Bible Study

The points outlined above on how to search for truth are simple, and "blessed is he that *readeth* and they that hear the words of this prophecy and keep those things which are written therein" (Revelation 1:3, italics supplied). If it is so simple, why do men make it complicated by studying the Bible through some scheme, as did Augustine (A.D. 354–430), a Champion of Christianity in Search of Truth, during the early Christian period. Augustine accepted the scheme of a *persona non-grata*, a schismatic Donatist, named Tichonius, as he himself acknowledges:

> One Tichonius, who although a Donatist himself,...wrote a book which he called the Book of Rules, because in it he laid down seven rules, which are, as it were, keys to open the secrets of Scripture.[1]

In Augustine's *magnum opus*, "The City of God," the "seven rules" of Tichonius are well applied, whereby the "millennium" of Revelation twenty is shifted back by "recapitulation" (Rule 6) to the first coming of Christ instead of commencing at the second coming. Rule 5 is predominant, leading from all reality and literal sense to fanciful, symbolic or mystical interpretations. One example will suffice to illustrate such allegorical interpretation, wherein the natural sense is given a meaning, other than what it conveys. Augustine says the words of Revelation 20, verse 9:

> 'And *fire* came down from God out of heaven, and devoured them,' *are not to be understood of the final punishment* which shall be inflicted when it is said, 'Depart from me, ye cursed, into everlasting fire;...In this place 'fire out

> of heaven' is well understood of the firmness of the saints, wherewith they refuse to yield obedience to those who rage against them. For the firmament is 'heaven' by whose firmness these assailants shall be *pained with blazing zeal*.[2]
>
> *(Italics supplied).*

Strange that literal devouring *fire*, is made to mean the *blazing zeal* of the saints, that consumes the wicked. Yet, *allegorical* interpretation became victorious under Augustine, and his acceptance of the "seven rules" of Tichonius led also to a system of "multiple interpretation," evinced in the treatise, "The City of God." In fact, the "seven rules" of Tichonius prevailed and molded *prophetic exposition for seven centuries*, until a reversal of the Tichonian tradition took place in the twelfth century, particularly under Joachim of Floris, Italy (Appendix A).

Allegorical interpretation has plagued many seekers of truth through the centuries. Even the Augustinian monk, Martin Luther, a Champion of Christianity in Search of Truth, declared: "I allegorized everything." He went on to say:

> I was thoroughly drilled in this method when I first began to study the Bible ten years ago, before I discovered the *true method*. I too would carelessly say: 'In the beginning God created heaven and earth' (Genesis 1:1): Heaven refers to the angels and the spiritual creatures; earth refers to the bodily creatures.
>
> *(Italics supplied)*

When Luther abandoned the *allegorical* method of interpretation for the *literal* sense of the text, while preparing his lectures on the epistle to the Romans, he indicated that this was an important change in his life. So important, that he understood "the true meaning of Christ's work did not lie in allegorizing about Him."[3]

7 Dispensations for Bible Study

Although the "seven rules" of Tichonius are not around today, allegorical interpretation is still prevalent. But, what is more alarming today, are seven popular keys to open the secrets of Scripture—the "seven dispensations," a scheme systematized in the nineteenth century by John Darby of the Plymouth Brethren, Great Britain.

In America the "seven dispensations" was popularized by the Scofield Reference Bible, first copyrighted in 1909. This dispensational framework divides world history into seven periods, exhibiting the supposed progressive order of God's dealings with humanity, having significance for the people of that period alone, and for no one else. The dispensational approach to Bible study is divisive, since it divides the Bible into virtually two books:

(1) The Book of the Kingdom, comprising the Old Testament and the Synoptic Gospels addressed to Jews only, who are under the dispensation of LAW;

(2) The Book of the Church, comprising the Epistles addressed to Christians since the crucifixion, who are under the dispensation of GRACE.

Such dispensational study of Scripture deprives the Christian of the Old Testament, as stigmatized under law. Yet Paul indicated that Old Testament happenings are for our admonition today, stating Israel "did all drink the same spiritual drink: for they drank of that spiritual Rock that followed them: and that Rock was Christ. Now all these things happened unto them for ensamples: and they are written for our admonition, upon whom the ends of the world are come" (1 Corinthians 10:4,11).

Furthermore, the dispensational framework deprives the Christian of many of the *most sublime teachings of Christ*, because Christ is said to be under the *dispensation of law*, and therefore was *addressing Jews only*; "nothing indeed was addressed to the church by the Lord in person, because the church did not yet exist to be addressed" so runs the line from John Darby.[4]

Thus, the Sermon on the Mount is seen as "legal in character" through the dispensational framework. When Jesus said, "If you love me keep my commandments" (John 14:15) or "The sabbath was made for man" (Mark 2:27), that is through dispensational eyes—*extreme legalism, fit for the Jews, but not applicable to Christians*. But, I thought the definition of a Christian is one who follows Christ and His teachings. For did not Jesus say: "Go ye therefore, and teach all nations, baptizing them...Teaching them to observe all things whatsoever I have commanded you" (Matthew 28:19,20).

Dispense with the dispensational prism of "seven dispensations" when reading the Bible, and realize the simple fact, that world history is covered by one dispensation—GRACE. The *prot-evangelium* (the first gospel) is found in Genesis 3, verse 15. Paul teaches Abraham and David were saved "without works" by "imputed righteousness" (Romans 4:1–8; Galatians 3:1–8; Genesis 15:6; Psalms 32:1,2). Hebrews, chapter eleven, inscribes a number of Old Testament characters on the honor roll of faith or grace.

HOW TO SEARCH FOR TRUTH IN PROPHECY

Understanding the element of Bible prophecy is clearly enunciated by Jesus: "I have told you before it comes to pass, that, when it is come to pass, ye might believe" (John 14:29). In other words Jesus states the prophecy, but one may not understand and believe it until its fulfillment. Or, the closer one comes to the time of fulfillment, the more one understands the prophecy. But, the recognition of fulfillment at the exact time it comes to pass, will strengthen one's belief in divine forecast.

"We have also a more sure word of prophecy; whereunto ye do well that ye take heed, as unto a light that shineth in a dark place, until the day dawn, and the day star arise in your hearts" (2 Peter 1:19,20).

This principle enunciated by Peter, shows there is a gradual unfolding of prophecy down through time, like the faint glimmer of light in darkness, until the day dawns dispelling the darkness—until the clear full light of understanding bursts in upon the mind, like the arising of the day star. Therefore, there is an uninterrupted progression of prophecy toward the goal of fulfillment.

What about interpretation of prophecy? Peter says, "no prophecy of Scripture is of any private interpretation" (2 Peter 1:20). That rules out any "multiple interpretations." The Bible is its own expositor and therefore prophecy interprets itself. We find this so, with the apocalyptic or eschatological outline prophecies of Daniel and Revelation. Daniel himself says "we will tell the interpretation" (Daniel 2:36) of the metallic statue, and that the four metals of the statue describe the rise of three consecutive "kingdoms" after Babylon (See Daniel 2:39,40). Likewise, the parallel prophecy of Daniel 7 explains the symbols of the beasts: "These great beasts which are four, are four kings, which shall arise out of the earth" (Daniel 7:17).

The purpose of prophecy is not only to reveal "what shall be in the latter days" or "what should come to pass hereafter" (Daniel 2:28,29), but also to speak to God's people in every age spanning all time. It is also an incentive "looking for and hastening unto the coming of the day of God...look for new heavens and a new earth wherein dwelleth righteousness. Wherefore, beloved, seeing that ye look for such things, be diligent that ye may be found of him in peace, without spot, and blameless" (2 Peter 3:12–14).

"He which testifieth these things saith, Surely I come quickly, Amen. Even so come Lord Jesus" (Revelation 22:20).

Postscript. For further elaboration on the Simple Rule for Bible Study, See Appendix C.

(1)

A GUIDED TOUR IN SEARCH OF TRUTH (PART 1)

Shalom—Peace be unto you! May I have the privilege to take you on a guided tour?

Come with me and I will be your guide and lecturer on an intriguing tour of the Monuments of Christianity in our search for truth. By far the most attractive monument will be seen in the "eternal city" Rome as we wend our way down the Via della Conciliazione and stand in awe before Saint Peter's cathedral. Michelangelo's genius was lavished on the design of the cupola or dome of Saint Peter's to dazzle the human eye—what a breathtaking spectacle to pause at and wonder.

But, we must amble through the *piazza* of Saint Peter's, encircled, enfolded, if not embraced by the giant arms of Bernini's colonnade, representing the loving embrace of the Prince of the Apostles. Or, if we happen to assemble in the *piazza*, with the growing crowd on a certain day, we may receive the embrace of the pope giving the blessing—"Urbi et Orbi" (to the city and the world).

We are about to enter the magnificent basilica of Saint Peter's, that was consecrated thirteen centuries after the original Constantinian basilica was consecrated. Pope Julius II resolved to build a splendid monument over the tomb of the first pope—a veritable gem in the crown of the church, and a worthy temple on earth of the Universal Church of Christ.

We enter the vestibule of Saint Peter's and are greeted by equestrian statues at each end, of the imperial protectors of the church and papacy: Constantine the Great and Charlemagne.

Charlemagne

Near the central bronze door we view a large red porphyry slab inserted in the pavement. Emperors and kings knelt upon it, to kiss the cross and recite the creed, before going to the tomb of the apostle Peter to be anointed and crowned. On this stone Charlemagne was crowned in splendor, Christmas day A.D. 800, and became the first emperor of the Holy Roman Empire, that was to last a thousand years, until abolished by Napoleon. Nevertheless, since authority was vested in the succeeding emperors by the church through coronation, the greater authority was the church, the emperors mere puppets in the church's hands.

Focal-point: The Confession

Step into the vast basilica of Saint Peter's, decorated left and right with statues of standing, kneeling, and reclining popes; replete with tombs and more altars than any church on earth, where Jesus is sacrificed, and the bread and wine are changed into His body and blood by transubstantiation. Look straight ahead, across the vast nave to the Confession that covers the tomb of Peter, above which is the papal altar, and rising still higher, the splendid canopy supported by Bernini's spiral columns.

Humiliation of Canossa

There's still more splendor to behold, but let's walk down the right aisle. Notice the tomb with reliefs depicting the Humiliation of Canossa, A.D. 1077. Pope Gregory VII is shown absolving Henry IV, mighty emperor of Germany and Italy, who had obstinately disobeyed the pope. However, absolution came only after Henry had done penance, waiting three days bareheaded and barefooted, standing ankle deep in snow, at the fortress Canossa, in Tuscany, Italy. Suffice it to say, that papal political power was well nigh culminated in the reign of pope Gregory.

Leo the Great

Let's shake a leg, and hurry on to the top of the left aisle of Saint Peter's, and stop at the chapel of pope Leo the Great (A.D. 440–461). Leo laid the early foundation of that stupendous institution—the papacy, that towered among the nations for over a thousand years. First, Leo protested the equal privilege of the see of Constantinople with the see of Rome, as decided by the Council of Chalcedon, A.D. 451. Leo claimed that he, the bishop of Rome, ought to be supreme; since the bishop of Rome was the official "guardian of the Catholic faith, and of the traditions of the fathers."

Second, after the sack of Rome by Alaric the Goth, A.D. 410, Leo courageously approached the "scourge of God," Attila the Hun, and persuaded him to retreat from Italy in 452. Thus, Leo won for himself, and the church, great respect and prestige—a powerful protector, entering the role of arbiter of the nations, to be continued by his successors.

We must leave the chapel of pope Leo the Great, depicting Leo's meeting Attila, exhibited in a large bold relief, and ponder if there are any other factors that propelled Leo and his successors. Yes there are! And that takes us to the next stop in our tour of Saint Peter's.

Saint Peter's Statue

We follow the pilgrims passing by the bronze seated statue of Saint Peter. And as they pass by, they fondle or kiss the toe of the extended right foot. The toe has been smoothed by the fondling and kisses of millions of pilgrims, and you may wish to add a shine to it. (See Photo 1).

Photo 1
Statue of Saint Peter
on the Feast of St. Peter

If you arrive there on the feast of Saint Peter, the statue is vested in a cope of gold brocade, and crowned with a jeweled tiara, normally housed in the Treasury of Saint Peter's. The tiara has great significance—for it is the crown of popes. It is called the "triple crown" and means the wearer of it, is "king of heaven and of earth, and of the lower regions."[1]

Papal succession

You have seen a number of things at eye-level, but stand by the Confession, throw your head back, and lift your eyes upward looking two hundred feet up into the dome (See Photo 2). The dome is as wide as the pantheon, and running round it, in black mosaic letters, five feet tall, on a gold ground are Latin words meaning in English:

> Thou art Peter and upon this Rock I will build my church
> and the gates of hell shall not prevail against it.
>
> *Matthew 16:18.*

Photo 2
"Tu Es Petrus—Thou Art Peter"
These words of Christ, that embellish the inside of the dome of St. Peter's, constitute the Papacy's greatest claim to primacy and papal succession.

It is claimed in this text, that Christ's statement to Peter made the apostle Christ's successor, or vicar of Christ, or His vicegerent, the visible and infallible head of the church. Further, that Christ built His church upon Peter, making Peter the foundation of His church. Second, it is claimed that Peter was the first bishop or pope of the church in the city of Rome. Therefore this privilege and power was handed down in succession, to all the bishops, or popes of that imperial city.

Dr. Martin Luther challenged Dr. John Eck in the Leipzig debate regarding "papal succession," showing that the church was not founded upon Peter, "for other foundation can no man lay than that is laid, which is Jesus Christ" (1 Corinthians 3:11). Therefore to deny that Christ is the head and foundation of the church is a DEPARTURE FROM CHRIST.

Even the church doctor, Augustine, writing in Retractions, 1:21, gave the correct interpretation of Jesus statement to Peter:

> For it was not said to him 'Thou art the rock' (*petra*), but 'Thou art Peter' (*petros*). For Christ was the rock whom Simon confessing, as the whole church confesses Him.

The distinction is clear that rock (petra) and Peter (petros) are not one and the same thing. Petra is a rock of large dimensions—a feminine substantive. Petros, on the other hand, is a small or rolling stone—a masculine noun. Christ would not build His church upon a rolling stone, but upon Himself a firm rock foundation.

Looking closely at Matthew 16, verse 18, containing Jesus statement to Peter, we see nothing to indicate that if Peter was to be the head of the church, that this privilege would be handed down in succession for all time. There is no "papal succession" or inherited privilege enunciated.

Where did the doctrine of the primacy of Peter and papal succession come from? Dr. John Eck in the Leipzig debate with Martin Luther, appealed to history to substantiate the claim. But, what he produced, were forgeries. They were fabricated sayings of earlier popes, and decisions of earlier councils, incorporated into the Isidorian Decretals of the ninth century.

Luther cried out to Dr. Eck in the debate, "I impugn these decretals." Luther was right, having done his homework in historical criticism, before knowing that Lorenzo Valla had proved the decretals spurious already.

Thus, Petrine primacy and papal succession was supported by forgeries, and not by history. Not even the church fathers gave the slightest hint to it from their study of the Scripture, as noted by the Roman Catholic theologian J.J. Dollinger:

> Of all the Fathers who interpret these passages in the Gospels, not a single one of them applies them to the Roman bishops as Peter's successors.[2]

Final Focal-Point: Altar of the Chair

Besides what has been discussed above, there were other factors that propelled the so-called successors of Saint Peter, and that takes us to the final spot in our tour of Saint Peter's. High in the apse we come across the Altar of the Chair, over which are the Latin doctors Augustine and Ambrose, and the Greek doctors Athanasius and Chrysostom, triumphantly supporting a bronze throne—*cathedra*. (See Photo 3).

Photo 3
Altar of the Chair, St. Peter's
Holy Doctors: Augustine, Ambrose, Athanasius, and Chrysostom, are depicted supporting the bronze throne—cathedra, symbolic seat of the Papacy.

The Altar of the Chair is full of symbolism, that has had a 'Chair within the Chair,' purportedly of Saint Peter, and used by him when preaching. The bronze throne—cathedra, represents the seat of the papacy, for the successors of Saint Peter. The four doctors of the church, noble quartet of fathers, support the papacy, and contribute to its elevation. But, one of them, namely Augustine, developed the framework for the elevation through his treatise, "The City of God."

"The City of God"

Following the sack of Rome, A.D. 410, Augustine entered into a correspondence with two Roman officials on the relation of the church and the empire. It seems, that out of such reflections, he conceived the concept of the "City of God," a blueprint for his church, the compilation of which spanned thirteen years. Sensing the collapse of Rome, Augustine, opportunist that he was, seized the opportunity to portray the "church militant" and victorious over the empire. Augustine injected a new philosophy of history with an extravagant exaltation of the church, and this concept fastened itself upon the church for well over a thousand years. The popularity of the "City of God" is attested by the publication of some twenty editions in pre-Reformation times, from 1467 to 1500.

Apart from introducing a new philosophy of history, Augustine introduced a new era in prophetic interpretation, by going wild with allegorical interpretation, and applying the "seven rules" of Tichonius (See Introduction). He set upon the twentieth chapter of Revelation on the millennium, and instead of taking the fulfillment of the millennium (thousand years) after the Second Coming, as believed by him and many Christians, he conveniently shifted it back (by Tichonian Rule 6) to the First Coming, and placed his present day church in the setting of the millennium. He even applied all the facets of the millennium to his church as: the kingdom of God—the kingdom of glory—the city of God—the New Jerusalem (Revelation 21:1–3). On the camp of the saints at Revelation 20, verse 9, Augustine made this preposterous claim to fit his theme:

> This camp is nothing else than the Church of Christ extending over the whole world....

Augustine contradicts the plain sense of Revelation 20, verse 4, describing the last judgment thus:

> Therefore the church even *now* is the kingdom of Christ, and the kingdom of heaven. Accordingly even *now* his saints reign with him....
>
> 'And I saw seats, and them that sat upon them, and judgment was given.' *It is not to be supposed* that this refers to

> the last judgment, but to the seats of the rulers themselves by whom the church is now governed.[3]

(Italics supplied).

Augustine misapplied the words of Jesus: "Compel them to come in" (Luke 14:23), in appealing to the secular arm to suppress the schismatic Donatists of his day, to despoil them of their churches and of their goods. This is a DEPARTURE FROM CHRIST.

This principle of forcible coercion threw a dark shadow over the glorious church concept he championed, when his writings later became the "Bible of the Inquisition" and the sanction for massacre.

Daniel, Chapter 2

Before considering another thought that Augustine injected into his concept of the "City of God," let us pause at the Altar of the Chair and familiarize ourselves with a passage of Scripture. Follow me on a guided tour through Daniel, Chapter two, in our search for truth:

> v. 28. But there is a God in heaven who reveals secrets, and He has made known to King Nebuchadnezzar what will be in the latter days. Your dream, and the visions of your head upon your bed, were these:
>
> v. 31. You, O King were watching; and behold, a great image! This great image, whose splendor was excellent, stood before you; and its form was awesome.
>
> v. 32. This image's head was of fine gold, its chest and arms of silver, its belly and thighs of bronze,
>
> v. 33. its legs of iron, its feet partly of iron and partly of clay.
>
> v. 34. You watched while a stone was cut out without hands, which struck the image on its feet of iron and clay, and broke them in pieces.
>
> v. 35. Then the iron, the clay, the bronze, the silver, and the gold were crushed together, and became like chaff from the summer threshing floors; the wind carried them away so that no trace of them was found. And the stone that struck the image became a great mountain and filled the whole earth.
>
> v. 36. This is the dream. Now we will tell the interpretation of it before the king.
>
> v. 37. You, O king, are a king of kings. For the God of heaven has given you a kingdom, power, strength, and glory;

v. 38.... you are this head of gold.

v. 39. But after you shall arise another kingdom inferior to yours; then another a third kingdom of bronze, which shall rule over all the earth.

v. 40. And the fourth kingdom shall be as strong as iron, inasmuch as iron breaks in pieces and shatters all things; and like iron that crushes, that kingdom will break in pieces and crush all the others.

v. 41. Whereas you saw the feet and toes, partly of potter's clay and partly of iron, the kingdom shall be divided; yet the strength of the iron shall be in it, just as you saw the iron mixed with ceramic clay.

v. 42. And as the toes of the feet were partly of iron and partly of clay, so the kingdom shall be partly strong and partly fragile.

v. 43. As you saw iron mixed with ceramic clay, they will mingle with the seed of men; but they will not adhere to one another, just as iron does not mix with clay.

v. 44. And in the days of these kings the God of heaven will set up a kingdom which shall never be destroyed; and the kingdom shall not be left to other people; it shall break in pieces and consume all these kingdoms, and it shall stand forever.

v. 45. Inasmuch as you saw that the stone was cut out of the mountain without hands, and that it broke in pieces the iron, the bronze, the clay, the silver, and the gold—the great God has made known to the king what will come to pass after this. The dream is certain, and its interpretation is sure.

The New King James Version

Let us note the main features of the dream given by God to King Nebuchadnezzar II—whose existence ancient history confirms.

Verse 28 says God made known to the king "what will be in the latter days"—that is in the future. Thus, stating that this dream is a prophecy.

Verses 31 to 35 describe the content of the dream. The king saw a metallic image or statue, comprising head of gold, chest and arms of silver, belly and thighs of bronze, legs of iron, and feet of iron and clay mixed together. Next, the king saw a stone strike the image and pulverize it—thereafter, growing into a mountain, and filling the whole earth.

Verse 36 states conclusively—"This is the dream. Now we will tell the interpretation." Thus, the principle is established, that "no prophecy of the

Scripture is of any private interpretation" (2 Peter 1:20). The Bible is its own expositor.

Verses 37 to 45, Daniel himself gives the interpretation, declaring that the head of gold represents King Nebuchadnezzar II, proud monarch of the kingdom of Neo-Babylon (B.C. 605–539), in the words: "You are this head of gold" (verse 38). Then after Neo-Babylon would "arise another kingdom" followed consecutively by a "third" and "fourth" kingdom. But, the fourth kingdom shall be as strong as iron. Then it "shall be divided," just like the feet of iron and clay are divided. Yet, the elements of division in the iron and clay will try to unite—"they will mix with one another in marriage" (verse 43, R.S.V.; see also Living Bible).

Finally, while the nations comprising the divided state, sometimes strong as iron, sometimes weak as clay, use all their power and ingenuity to unite—"they will not adhere to one another, just as iron does not mix with clay" (verse 43). Instead, "in the days of these kings the God of heaven will set up a kingdom which shall never be destroyed" (verse 44). God's kingdom is represented by the stone that destroyed the metallic image, and grew into a great mountain (verse 45). Such is the certainty of the dream and "its interpretation is sure" (verse 45).

The divine forecast of Daniel, Chapter two spans the ages—from Nebuchadnezzar's kingdom, through *three* successive kingdoms and a *divided* kingdom, to the setting up of the *stone kingdom* of God. But, the prophecy does not identify the intervening kingdoms. History identifies them, and Augustine leaned to their identity:

> Some have interpreted these four kingdoms as signifying those of the Assyrians, Persians, Macedonians, and Romans. They who desire to understand the fitness of this interpretation may read Jerome's book on Daniel, which is written with a sufficiency of care and erudition.[4]

Where Augustine slipped, is that while he recognized the fourth kingdom of iron as the Roman empire, he bypassed the "divided" state of the Roman empire, which would follow its collapse. Then he shifted back the stone kingdom of God (by Tichonian rule 6) to fit into his millennial existence of the city of God, presently manifested in his church of God. The imperial universal church from the first Coming of Christ, was to Augustine the stone shattering all earthly kingdoms, until according to Augustine it: "filled the whole earth." Instead of the stone kingdom of Christ being established at the Second Coming, Augustine shifted it back to the First Coming, thereby wresting the Scriptures.

On the other hand, Augustine from his perspective, had not witnessed the division and disintegration of the Roman power. It was still future to him, it only took place after A.D. 476. Nevertheless, in his interpretation he should not have bypassed the divided state of Rome, even if he could not explain it. Thus, we are more able to understand and believe prophecy as it unfolds in fulfillment, and we can look back. It is easier to understand fulfilled prophecy than unfulfilled prophecy.

Luther's Exposition

From the vantage point of Martin Luther over a thousand years later, here is his exposition:

> The first kingdom is the Assyrian or Babylonian kingdom; the second the Medo-Persian; the third the great kingdom of Alexander and the Greeks; and the fourth, the Roman Empire. In this the whole world agrees, and history supports it fully in detail. But the prophet has the most to say about the Roman empire,...the legs, the feet, and the toes. The Roman empire will be divided. Spain, France, England, and others emerged from it, some of them weak, others strong, and although it will be divided there will be some strength, as symbolized by the iron in it.... This empire shall last until the end; no one will destroy it but Jesus Himself, when His kingdom comes.[5] (See Illustration 1).

Luther was right, and may I add, that from our twentieth century perspective, we too are living in the divided stage of European nations that emerged from the division of Rome. In this divided stage some time soon, "in the days of these kings the God of heaven will set up a kingdom which shall never be destroyed" (Daniel 2:44).

Although Luther saw the divided stage of Rome "come to pass" that he "might believe" (John 14:29), there were theologians who closed their eyes to the fulfillment of the divided kingdoms of Rome, and opposed Luther, contending for the stone kingdom already established from Christ's first coming, as taught by Augustine, a thousand years before.

Augustine's concept of the church of God, reigning as the *millennial kingdom* and the *stone kingdom* of God, was to be materialized by pope Leo the Great and his successors, through pope Gregory VII and beyond. Likewise, Charlemagne, who loved to read Augustine's "City of God," gave strength to the concept of the Holy Roman Empire. Hence, the spiritual and the material empire was blended into a religio-political world-empire, with dominion over the consciences of men, when papal "bulls," instead of imperial decrees were to rule the world.

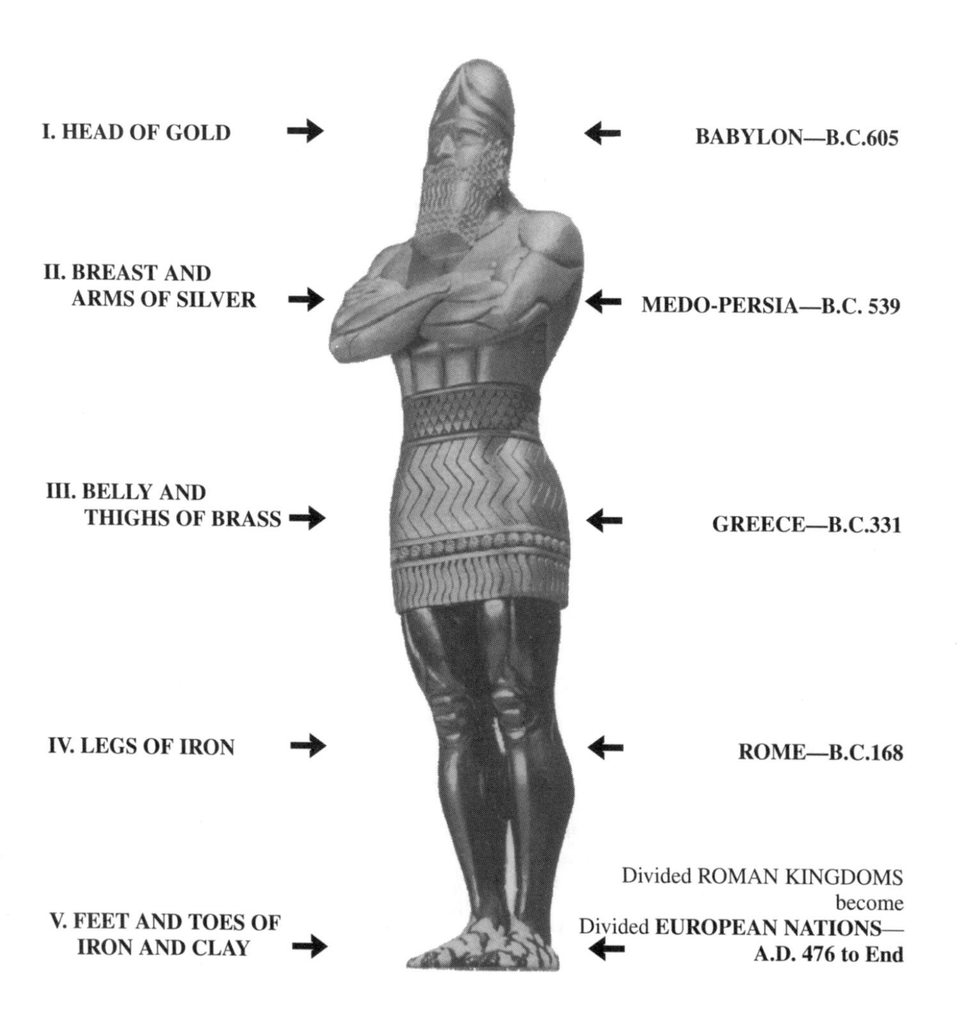

Illustration 1

The Metallic Statue of Daniel, Chapter Two

This illustrates the successive rise and fall of kingdoms, showing that we are in the divided stage of European nations. The dates indicate the successive conquests of one kingdom after another.

It is no wonder then, that when Luther saw the extreme, to which Augustine's concept had led, he declared:

> It is a horrible thing to behold the man who styles himself Christ's vicegerent, displaying a magnificence that no emperor can equal.... He is say they, the *lord of the world.* But Christ...has said, 'My kingdom is not of this world.' Can the dominions of a vicar extend beyond those of His superior?[6]
>
> *(Italics supplied).*

Several times Luther thundered those words of Jesus: "My kingdom is not of this world" (John 18:36). Therefore Augustine's concept is a denial of Jesus concept—a DEPARTURE FROM CHRIST. Jesus taught about a *future* kingdom of glory: "When the Son of Man shall come in his glory, and all the holy angels with him, then shall He sit upon the throne of His glory" and say "inherit the kingdom prepared for you" (Matthew 25:31,34)—that is the *stone kingdom.*

Kingdom of Grace

There is a difference between the future "kingdom of glory" and the present "kingdom of grace." The kingdom of grace is expressed as "the kingdom of God is within you" (Luke 17:21), also called the "gospel of the kingdom" (Matthew 24:14). Will it surprise you to discover, that Augustine had some concept of grace, that was greater than all the other church fathers? Had the church picked up on this teaching, how different would have been the historical course of the church. Surprise! Surprise! Ironically, the one who was influenced to some degree by Augustine's glimpse of grace, was none other than the Augustinian monk, Martin Luther, whose watch word was *sola gratia*—salvation by grace alone.

With that thought in mind we leave the Altar of the Chair, walk back all the way along the right-hand aisle of Saint Peter's, and view the magnificent sculpture—Michaelangelo's Pieta. The transverse limp body of the crucified Jesus, across the lap of Mary, reminds us: "Neither is there salvation in any other" (Acts 4:12), than in Jesus, whom God exalted to be a "Prince and a Savior," to give "forgiveness of sins" (Acts 5:31). "For by grace are ye saved through faith; and that not of yourselves: it is the gift of God: Not of works, lest any man should boast" (Ephesians 2:8,9).

As we leave Saint Peter's I want to drop in a commercial. I am sure that when Augustine wrote "The City of God," he did not visualize the extreme to which his concept would go. In all sincerity, he loved his church so much, that he wanted to extend its glory. The only mistake he made was to apply the "seven rules" of Tichonius, which among others, led to allegorical interpretation. But, let me announce that he read another prophecy at face value, that will astound, surprise, or shock the reader. Watch for it in Chapter 3!

Reformation Monument

From the Monument of Saint Peter's in Rome we wing our flight across the snowcapped Alps and land in Geneva, Switzerland. We seek out the University of Geneva—originally the College et l'Academie of John Calvin, that was one of the triumphs of the Protestant Reformation for training preachers. Close to the University we come across the Reformation Monument. It is a staunch stone wall three hundred feet long, featuring a central sculpture of four commanding clerical figures, flanked by a series of bas reliefs, tableaux, texts and smaller statues. These include for America: the voyage of the Pilgrims, the Mayflower Compact and a statue of Roger Williams. For Great Britain: John Knox preaching to the court of Mary Stuart, the Bill of Rights and a statue of Oliver Cromwell. For France: Admiral Coligny of the Huguenots. For the world's Christians: the Lord's Prayer. (See Photo 4 and 4a).

From the quartet of holy fathers at the Altar of the Chair in Saint Peter's, we now stand before the Reformation quartet, central to the wall of the Reformation Monument. The majestic quartet is made up of:

(1) Farel, who introduced the Reformation to Geneva and joined hands with the Waldenses;

(2) Calvin, who in due course became the leading theologian of Reformed Protestantism, through his great "Institutes of Christian Religion," and molded the reformation principle into a system of government and a way of life;

(3) Beza, assistant to Calvin in the reform movement;

(4) John Knox, reformer of Scotland and a founder of the Church of Scotland, who directed a new translation of the Bible into English, the so-called Geneva Bible or "Breeches Bible." The Geneva Bible, almost reverenced in Scotland, went through two hundred printings, until superseded by the King James version, on whose form its influence is evident.

Luther Memorial

From the Reformation quartet at the wall of the Reformation Monument in Geneva, the virtual center for the spread of the Reformation, we hasten to the Luther Memorial in Worms, Germany, and gaze at the Pre-Reformation quartet. Positioned on each corner of a square base pedestal are the statues of the Pre-Reformation quartet. From the center of the base pedestal rises a high pedestal, surmounted by an erect statue of Martin Luther. Surrounding this central statue complex are statues of Melanchthon and other German supporters of Luther. (See Photo 5, 5a & 5b).

We focus our attention on the Pre-Reformation quartet comprising:

Photo 4
Above: ***Reformation Monument, Geneva, Switzerland***
The 300 foot wall of figures and scenes reflect
the Protestant Reformation. The central sculpture features the Reformation quartet: Farel, Calvin, Beza, and Knox.

Photo 4a
Below: ***Exploded View***

Photo 5
Luther Memorial, Worms, Germany
The commanding figure of Martin Luther is surrounded on the outer edges of the Monument by his contemporary supporters.

Photo 5a
Beneath Luther is the
Pre-Reformation quartet*:*
Savonarola and Huss in front, with Waldo and Wycliffe behind.

Photo 5b
Peter Waldo
seated at the base of the Monument behind Martin Luther.

(1) Peter Waldo of Lyons, France, who fired up the Waldenses with missionary zeal;

(2) John Wycliffe, brilliant Oxford professor, described as the Morning Star of the Reformation. He organized a body of itinerant preachers and a substantial following known as Lollards, besides coming out with the first English version of the Bible around 1382;

(3) John Huss, from the University of Prague, the central figure of the Bohemian Reformation, who was burned at the stake for his faith in 1415;

(4) Girolamo Savonarola, of Florence, Italy, a fearless preacher of righteousness, the greatest spiritual force in Italy for the fifteenth century, who was hanged on the gallows and burned (1488) for identifying the Roman church with the harlot Babylon (Revelation 17).

"Here I Stand"

A little walk away from the Luther Memorial brings us to the spot marked by a plate with the words, "Here I stand." We recall the gallant stand made by Luther before the Diet:

> Unless I am convinced by Scripture and plain reason—I do not accept the authority of popes and councils, for they have contradicted each other—my conscience is captive to the Word of God. I cannot and I will not recant anything, for to go against conscience is neither right nor safe. Here I stand, I cannot do otherwise. May God help me. Amen.

I have introduced you to several quartets, the quartet of holy fathers, the Reformation quartet, together with the Pre-Reformation quartet. It is from these quartets, that I will select the players, together with several other single players still to be selected, to make up my cast in the drama of the ages.

These actors will take part in two Biblical plays, actually two divine forecasts: the Drama of the Apocalyptical Beasts (Daniel 7) and the Drama of the Woman and the Dragon (Revelation 12).

(2)

A GUIDED TOUR IN SEARCH OF TRUTH (PART 2)

Our guided tour of Monuments of Christianity in our search for truth, will take an unusual turn. Usually monuments are arranged with statues of people. But, we are going to visit monuments of Biblical plays—divine forecasts. The first one is the monument of the Drama of the Apocalyptical Beasts, and that takes us to the city of Nuremberg, Germany. Remember, Nuremberg was the venue for the Nazi war trials. Well, for our tour, it will be the focal point for the trial of truth.

Daniel, Chapter 7

But, before we visit the monument of the Drama of the Apocalyptical Beasts, let's read about that drama from Daniel, Chapter seven:

> v. 2. Daniel spoke, saying, 'I saw in my vision by night, and behold, the four winds of heaven were stirring up the great sea.
>
> v. 3. 'And four great beasts came up from the sea, each different from the other.
>
> v. 4. 'The first was like a LION, and had eagles wings....
>
> v.5. 'And suddenly another beast, a second like a BEAR....
>
> v.6. 'After this I looked, and there was another, like a LEOPARD, which had on its back four wings of a bird. The beast also had four heads and dominion was given it.
>
> v.7. 'After this I saw in the night visions, and behold, a FOURTH BEAST, dreadful and terrible, exceedingly strong. It had huge IRON TEETH; it was devouring, breaking in pieces, and trampling the residue with its feet. It was different from all the beasts that were before it, and it had TEN HORNS.
>
> v.8. 'I was considering the horns, and there was ANOTHER HORN, A LITTLE ONE, coming up AMONG them, before whom three of the first horns were plucked up by the roots. And there, in this horn, were eyes like the eyes of a man, and a mouth speaking pompous words.'
>
> v. 17. 'Those great beasts, which are four, are FOUR KINGS which arise out of the earth.'
>
> v. 23. Thus he said:

'The FOURTH BEAST shall be a FOURTH KINGDOM on earth....

v. 24. The TEN HORNS ARE TEN KINGS who shall arise from this kingdom. And another shall arise AFTER them; He shall be DIFFERENT from the first ones, And shall subdue three kings.

v. 25. He shall speak POMPOUS words against the Most High, Shall PERSECUTE the saints of the Most High, And shall intend to CHANGE TIMES AND LAW. Then the saints shall be given into his hand For a TIME TIMES AND HALF A TIME.'

The New King James Version (Capitalization supplied)

Summary: Daniel 7

Here is a summary of Daniel 7. Daniel had a vision of the rise of four beasts, one after the other—beasts like a lion, a bear, a leopard and a fourth beast, unlike any animal on earth. The fourth beast was exceedingly strong, with iron teeth and ten horns. While Daniel considered the ten horns, there came up among them (verse 8), arising after them (verse 24), another "little horn," before whom three of the original ten horns were uprooted. This "little horn" was very animated with eyes and mouth, remarkably different (verse 24), "whose appearance was greater than his fellows" (verse 20). The "little horn" spoke pompous words against the Most High, persecuted the saints of the Most High, intended to change times and laws, and would have power over the saints for a time, times and half a time (verse 25).

Identity of 4 Beasts

Such is the Drama of the Apocalyptical beasts—but, what do the four beasts represent? Verse 17, says, "those great beasts which are four, are four kings which arise out of the earth." That parallels the four kingdoms of Daniel, chapter two, where they are mentioned by way of four metals in the metallic image. Note also the parallel in the *legs of iron* of the fourth kingdom in Daniel 2, with the *teeth of iron* of the fourth beast in Daniel 7. We have to conclude then, that the four beasts represent the four kingdoms: Neo-Babylon, Medo-Persia, Greece, Rome. (See Illustration 2).

Like Daniel, chapter two, the divine forecast of Daniel, chapter seven , spans the ages—from Neo-Babylon to Rome, through the ten horns and "little horn," until their demise, and the setting up of the "everlasting kingdom given to the saints of the Most High" (Daniel 7:26). But the prophecy does not identify the intervening ten horns and "little horn." Nevertheless, clues are given.

Illustration 2
Comparison of Prophecies of Daniel 2 and Daniel 7.

Identity of 10 Horns

Here are the clues. Verse 24 says, "the ten horns are ten kings who shall arise from this kingdom"—from the dreadful fourth beast with iron teeth, Rome. History accounts for the rise of ten kingdoms upon the dissolution and division of Rome: Ostrogoths, Visogoths, Franks, Vandals, Suevi, Alamanni, Anglo-Saxons, Heruli, Lombards, Burgundians. By the way, these kingdoms became the progenitors of the modern nations of Europe, for instance the Anglo-Saxons became the English, the Franks became the French, and so on. Remember, Luther enumerated some of these nations from Daniel 2.

Identity of the "Little Horn"

We follow up on the next clue, regarding the rise of the blasphemous "little horn," who would speak pompous words against the Most High, and persecute the saints of the Most High. This "little horn," would be "different" from the regular political horn kingdoms, and would in fact outshine them (verse 20). But, it would arise from "among" the ten kingdoms, and not beyond them, from their very midst—the cradle of Western Europe. The location of the rise of the "little horn" is vital. We cannot look for it to rise in the Middle-East or the Far-East, or any place else.

The next vital point is the time factor for the rise of the "little horn." Daniel says it shall arise "after" the ten kingdoms (verse 24). The official collapse of Rome from incursions brought on particularly by Goths, Vandals and finally Heruli, under Odoacer, was A.D. 476. Furthermore, the ten separate kingdoms were ultimately established by 476. So we have to look for the rise of the "little horn" after 476.

There is yet another point regarding the time for the rise of the "little horn," and that is, upon its rise "three of the first horns were plucked up by the roots" (verse 8). Looking at the Hammond Historical Atlas, 1960, the map on page H-8 entitled, "Europe 600 A.D.," shows seven of the kingdoms outlined above, but three are not there—namely the Ostrogoths, the Heruli and the Vandals. Therefore the "little horn" must arise between 476 and 600. Actually, Justinian effectively uprooted the last of these Arian kingdoms, when he despatched Belisarius, who drove the Ostrogoths from Rome in 538.[1]

Having pinpointed the rise of the "little horn" in the year 538 are we on the horns of a dilemma to identify the "little horn" power? So here's another Biblical clue. The little horn "shall be different" from the ten horns (verse 24). Horns denote political entities or kingdoms. This "little horn" must also be a political entity. But the verse says it is different. What makes the difference is that it is a religious power or rather a combination—a religio-political institution. Such an institution arose "among" the ten kingdoms, in the very midst of them, right on time, at the city of Rome—the Roman Papacy.

The American Catholic Quarterly Review, April, 1911 comments on the rise of the Roman Papacy:

> And meekly stepping to the throne of Caesar, the vicar of Christ took up the scepter to which the emperors and kings of Europe were to bow in reverence through so many centuries.

The celebrated historian H.G. Wells adds his comments:

> In a few centuries the Pope had become in theory, and to a certain extent in practice, the high priest censor, judge, and divine monarch of Christendom.[2]

Sufficient points of identity of the "little horn" have been noted, so here's a commercial, more is to follow in the next chapter. Further points will set the identity in concrete.[3]

Apocalyptical Beasts, Nuremberg

So let's proceed to the monument of the Drama of the Apocalyptical Beasts in Nuremberg, that will set the prophecy in concrete or stone, just like the ten commandments were written on stone. (See Photo 6, 6a & 6b).

Daniel's Quartet of Apocalyptical Beasts, Town Hall, Nuremberg, Germany

Photo 6
***Winged-Lion** (symbol of Neo-Babylon) **with Nebuchadnezzar II**, and **Cyrus with Bear** (symbol of Medo-Persia).*

Photo 6a
***Four-headed Leopard** (symbol of Greece) with Alexander the Great, and Julius Caesar with **Ten-horned Beast** (symbol of the Pagan Roman Empire).*

Photo 6b
*Among the ten horns, you can see the **Little Horn** with the animated face (symbol of Papal Rome).*

The almost three hundred foot long Rathaus or Town Hall of Nuremberg, scene of the diets of the empire, has three beautiful Doric portals. Over the two outer portals are the sculptures of the beasts authorized by the city council in 1617. Over the one portal is the Lion with Nebuchadnezzar, king of *Neo-Babylon*, and the Bear with Cyrus king of *Persia*. Over the other portal is the Leopard representing *Greece* with Alexander the Great, and the Ten-horned beast representing *Rome* with the emperor Julius Caesar. A close-up of the ten-horned beast reveals the "little horn" with a face representing the *Roman Papacy*.

Nuremberg

After Luther presented his Ninety-five Theses, Nuremberg was among the first towns sympathetic to Luther, and after the preaching of Andreas Osiander (1498–1552), Nuremberg stood solidly behind the Reformation. Gutenberg's press was introduced early in Nuremberg, and by the year 1500, there were twenty five printers destined to publish Bibles and many theological works.

The Reformer, Osiander

Osiander was the outstanding reformer in Nuremberg, proficient in mathematics, astronomy, medicine, and theology. He taught Hebrew in the Augustinian convent in Nuremberg. He was invited by Copernicus to make corrections to his epochal work, "On the Revolutions of the Celestial Spheres," for which Osiander wrote a preface. He wrote "A Harmony of the Gospels," at the request of Archbishop Cranmer of England, which was the first Protestant work of its kind. John Melanchthon asked Osiander to write a definitive work on the prophetic time periods of Daniel. Osiander's response was the book, "Conjectures Concerning the Last Times and the End of the World."

Osiander's "Conjectures," was putting it mildly, he hoped, "they were not far from the truth."[4] As best he could, Osiander applied the principles of grammatico-historical exegesis to the study of the Scriptures (See Appendix C). While Osiander gave clear-cut presentations on Daniel, chapter 7, and related passages, he dated the rise of the papacy from the sack of Rome by Alaric the Goth about 412, thereby not taking into account the rise of the "little horn" with the uprooting of the three Arian horns by 538. But, he was accurate in his understanding of the time period allotted to the little horn at Daniel seven, verse 25:

> Then the saints shall be given into his hand
> For a time and times and half a time.

Prophetic Time in Daniel and Revelation

Here is Osiander's statement on prophetic time periods verbatim:

> These are angelic years, or *prophetic time*. *Twelve hundred and sixty literal years* which are also mentioned in the 12th

> chapter of Revelation, where it is also mentioned as *a time, and times, and half a time.*[5]
>
> *(Italics supplied).*

Without going into the ramifications of equating the 1,260 days at Revelation 12, verse 6, with the parallel "a time and times and half a time" at Revelation 12, verse 14, Osiander applied the 1,260 symbolic days as 1,260 literal years to the little horn papacy. Thus, the papacy would have supreme authority over the saints of God—"they shall be given into his hand" for 1,260 years. Osiander dated the 1,260 years from 412, thereby ending papal dominance in 1672, followed by the end of the world soon thereafter (see Daniel 7:26).[6]

For the Drama of the Woman and the Dragon we will have to take a long flight from Nuremberg, Germany, to Cape Town, South Africa. You will be able to catch up on some reading, for this guided tour of the Monuments of Christianity, in our search for truth. So why not read Revelation, Chapter 12:

Revelation, Chapter 12

> v.1. Now a great sign appeared in heaven: a woman clothed with the sun, with the moon under her feet, and on her head a garland of twelve stars.
>
> v.2. Then being with child, she cried out in labor and in pain to give birth.
>
> v.3. And another sign appeared in heaven: behold a great, fiery red dragon having seven heads and ten horns, and seven diadems on his heads.
>
> v.4. His tail drew a third of the stars of heaven and threw them to the earth. And the dragon stood before the woman who was ready to give birth, to devour her Child as soon as it was born.
>
> v.5. And she bore a male Child who was to rule all nations with a rod of iron. And her Child was caught up to God and to His throne.
>
> v.6. Then the woman fled into the wilderness where she has a place prepared by God, that they should feed her there one thousand two hundred and sixty days.
>
> v.13. Now when the dragon saw that he had been cast to the earth, he persecuted the woman who gave birth to the male Child.
>
> v.14. But the woman was given two wings of a great eagle, that she might fly into the wilderness to her place, where she is nourished for a time and times and half a time from the presence of the serpent.

v. 15. So the serpent spewed water out of his mouth like a flood after the woman, that he might cause her to be carried away by the flood.

v. 16. But the earth helped the woman, and the earth opened its mouth and swallowed up the flood which the dragon had spewed out of his mouth.

v. 17. And the dragon was enraged with the woman, and he went to make war with the rest of her offspring, who keep the commandments of God and have the testimony of Jesus Christ.

The New King James Version

Summary: Revelation 12

A summary of Revelation, chapter twelve follows. The Drama of the Woman and the Dragon is like a Biblical version of Beauty and the Beast. The prophetic woman, clothed with the sun, and wearing a crown of twelve stars brings forth a child, while the dragon stands ready to destroy the child. The child is caught up to God and His throne, while the woman flees to the wilderness. Yet it is a place prepared by God for her protection, where she is nourished for 1,260 days. The drama then breaks off to describe the origin of the conflict in heaven and the expulsion of the dragon, or devil. The drama picks up once more at verse thirteen, when the devil who no longer has access to the courts of heaven, continues his conflict with the woman. Jesus had effected this eventual expulsion by His death on the cross, when His words were fulfilled, "I beheld satan as lightning fall from heaven (Luke 10:18; See also John 12:31).

Verse 14 of Revelation twelve repeats the woman fleeing into the wilderness. The devil continues to persecute the woman by spewing out a flood after her, but the earth helps the woman by absorbing the flood. Finally the devil goes after the rest of her offspring, or "remnant" (King James Version), to destroy them.

Exposition: Revelation 12

A lot of symbolic language is used in Revelation, chapter twelve, but without too much stretch of the imagination, the sense of the drama, suggests that the woman represents the Christian Church bringing forth Christ, who must be the person, who alone is caught up to God and to His throne. And if that is your understanding, you are in good company, because that has been the common understanding, starting with Victorinus, who died a martyr under Diocletian, about A.D. 304, and wrote the earliest systematic commentary on the Revelation.

But, if you are not clear, here are some texts of Scripture: "I have likened the daughter of Zion to a comely and delicate woman" (Jeremiah 6:2). Paul, addressing the Corinthian church said, "I have espoused you to one husband, that I may present you as a chaste virgin to Christ" (2 Corinthians 11:2). Revelation describes the final union of Christ with His church as the marriage supper of the Lamb: "and His wife hath made herself ready" by being "arrayed in fine linen, clean and white: for the fine linen is the righteousness of the saints" (Revelation 19:8). It is conclusive that a delicate, chaste woman, and a bride represent the pure Christian Church.

Now then, the woman or Christian church of Revelation twelve is "clothed with the sun" denoting her glory, purity and righteousness. She is clothed with Christ, who is the SUN OF RIGHTEOUSNESS (Malachi 4:2). Jesus also said, "I am the light of the world" (John 8:12).

This sun-clothed woman not only represents the New Testament Church, but *God's True Church down through the Christian era*. In contrast to the true church, Revelation seventeen portrays the existence of a *fallen* church that has departed from Christ, a "woman arrayed in purple and scarlet color, and decked with gold and precious stones and pearls, having a golden cup in her hand, full of abominations" and called "Babylon the Great" (Revelation 17:4,5).

Let's get back to the sun-clothed woman who enters the wilderness for 1,260 days. Since the woman is a symbol for the church, the wilderness is symbolic for a humiliating experience, also described as "clothed in sackcloth" (Revelation 11:3), barely existing, barely subsisting, being "nourished" by God. The devil sends out a "flood after the woman" in the form of inquisitors, crusades and massacres (See Isaiah 8:7; Jeremiah 46:8). Yes, that is persecution—papal persecution against the church in the wilderness.

Remember, one of the identifying marks of the little horn papacy was that it "shall persecute the saints of the Most High," and the "saints shall be given into his hand for" 1,260 years as noted by Osiander (Daniel 7:25). Therefore, the reason why the sun-clothed woman is in the wilderness for a parallel 1,260 years, is because she is being oppressed and persecuted by the papal little horn.

Nevertheless, during the wilderness experience the sun-clothed woman is helped. There are "places prepared by God" for her safety. The "earth helped the woman" can be taken as some of the great men of the earth helping. Others, see the great Protestant Reformation helping the woman. Still others, believe the literal earth of distant lands, such as the new world of America, opened its mouth and swallowed up the flood of oppression. All of these are plausible explanations.

The big question is who comprised the church in the wilderness? That will be answered later in this chapter, and in Chapter 4. And remember that the church in the wilderness spanned 1,260 years, and if we add that to A.D. 412 as did Osiander, that will bring us to 1672. Or, more accurately, if we add it to A.D. 538 that will take us to 1798. Then, after the church in the wilderness comes the Last Day Church or the "rest of her offspring" to the end of time, and Chapter 9 will be devoted to that subject. So, there are some wonderful revelations coming up—is that a good commercial? Stay tuned!

Cape Town, South Africa

With the Drama of the Woman and the Dragon from Revelation twelve clearly in mind, we land in Cape Town, South Africa. Cape Town is located on the southern tip of the great continent of Africa. The city is nestled at the foot of Table Mountain, which, on a clear day is covered with a table cloth of clouds. During the age of geographical discovery and exploration, that table was to furnish victuals for mariners of the Dutch East India Company, as they rounded the Cape en route to distant lands. Consequently, a revictualing station was established and colonized by the Dutch in 1652.

Since two oceans meet at Cape Town the sea can get rough—it was dubbed the "Cape of Storms." But, the prospects of the hinterland sought for change—it was then called the "Cape of Good Hope." It was the hope of a better life, free from the shackles of oppression and persecution, free to follow ones own religious convictions, that drew a batch of French Huguenots, to find asylum in fertile lands, not many miles beyond Table Mountain. It was to them "a place prepared by God," or the earth that "opened its mouth and swallowed up the flood" of oppression.

Huguenot Monument

So, to commemorate the arrival of the French Huguenots, and to express gratitude for their Protestant heritage, the Huguenot Monument and Museum was established at Fransch Hoek (See Photo 7).

The main feature of the Huguenot Monument, is the draped figure of a woman standing upon the world—prominently displaying Africa with the Cape embellished. The woman is depicted, casting off a cloak of oppression. The Bible in her right hand, and a broken chain in her left hand, symbolizes freedom of religious belief. She stands poised above the earth, her gaze is fixed on a noble vision of the future. Behind her are the symbols of her fortitude: three towering arches represent the Holy Trinity. Above the arches shines a depiction of the sun, representing the SUN OF RIGHTEOUSNESS. She represents the sun-clothed woman of Revelation 12.

Huguenot Identity with the Church in Wilderness

Why did the Huguenots choose the sun-clothed woman of Revelation twelve for their Monument? Because they identified themselves with the prophecy of the church in the wilderness. They saw themselves in the prophecy, and it spoke courage to them under privation, and satisfaction to know they constituted God's true church during that period.

I am sure that the hopes of the 150 Huguenots who arrived at the Cape of Good Hope were realized. For, not only had the literal "earth helped the

Photo 7

Huguenot Monument, Fransch Hoek, Cape, South Africa

The French Huguenots identified themselves with the true church: the metaphorical sun-clothed woman that fled from persecution to the wilderness (Revelation 12:6, 14). The metaphorical woman is depicted standing free above the world, with South Africa her wilderness refuge embellished. Above the arches is the depiction of the Sun of Righteousness (Revelation 12:1).

woman," but the Huguenots multiplied and replenished the earth" (Genesis 1:28). since they numbered 750 in twenty five years time.[7] And today over 300,000 South Africans can trace their surnames back to the Huguenots.

Revocation of Edict of Nantes, 1685

But, what precipitated the arrival of the Huguenots at the Cape in 1688? It was the Revocation of the Edict of Nantes, 1685, whereby King Louis XIV of France, with papal backing, decreed stringent measures for the specific extirpation of the Huguenots. Those who attempted to leave the country would be confined to lifelong slavery in the galleys, the women imprisoned, and property confiscated.

Mass Exodus

The Revocation of the Edict of Nantes precipitated a mass exodus, comparable to the Biblical exodus. Conservative estimates, put the number at 400,000 French Protestants who left France, and fled to Switzerland, Germany, Holland, England and America. Some historians estimate an equal number perished in prison, on the scaffold, at the galleys, or in their attempts to escape. "These atrocities were enacted...in no dark age, but the brilliant era of Louis XIV."[8]

Finer details of the mass exodus, show that 1,200 refugees passed Geneva in a week; over 600 refugees, one of the largest single arrivals landed in Virginia; New York Dutch Governor Stuyvesant invited Huguenots, who established the town of New Rochelle, near the shore of Long Island Sound, in memory of the Rochelle they left in France, that had been reduced from 27,000 to 5,000 inhabitants; the city of Boston admitted several hundred Huguenots; and so the story goes on.

While these details demonstrate how the sun-clothed woman found asylum in the new earth of America that "swallowed up the flood" of oppression, no great masses of French are found in the United States. The reason is that the French are less inclined to emigration than other people in Europe. Therefore, many of the Huguenots found asylum in the lands of Europe. But, still many Huguenots fled to southern France.

Eglise du Desert

For the best part of a century, the Huguenots, deprived of their pastors and their organization, resorted to southern France, there to meet in secret places in the mountains, in forests, in lonely moors, in caves and desolate places—in "places prepared by God." But, these French Protestants were "nourished" by God, when He raised Antoine Court to lead assemblies of worship. These assemblies culminated in their first Synod in 1715 at Cevennes—the very year in which Louis XIV declared that the Reformed Church was extinct. Antoine Court also established a Huguenot Seminary at Lausanne, Switzerland.

A distinct phase of French Protestantism developed, not only had the Huguenots identified themselves with the sun-clothed woman who went into the wilderness, but they actually named themselves EGLISE DU DESERT—CHURCH OF THE WILDERNESS. Even their baptismal and marriage certificates were dated from "The Wilderness."

Prior to the awful slaughter of 50,000 French Huguenots in the Massacre of St. Bartholomew, 1572, Admiral Coligny, gallant leader of the Huguenots, tried to establish a Huguenot colony at Parris Island, South Carolina, in 1562. This early enterprise at Charlesfort was abandoned, but after the Revocation of the Edict of Nantes, hundreds of Huguenot refugees arrived at Charleston, South Carolina. They built a church, and today one may visit the oldest Huguenot church in America dated from 1844. From a history of this Huguenot church in Charleston, I discovered that the last French Protestant colony to South Carolina, consisted of 138, under the leadership of Reverend J.L. Gibert in 1764. He was one of the pastors of EGLISE DU DESERT—CHURCH OF THE WILDERNESS[9] located in Charleston.

Large and varied groups of Christians belonged to the sun-clothed woman—the church in the wilderness, besides French Huguenots. These will be discussed later. But, for now let me say, that I have introduced to you the players and two Biblical plays, Daniel 7 and Revelation 12. These players and the Biblical plays will constitute the Drama of the Ages, as everything is played out in the rest of my book.

Christ of the Andes

Before we conclude our tour of Christian monuments, in search of truth, I take you from the Huguenot Monument in South Africa, to South America, for the monument known as "Christ of the Andes." It is located on the boundary between Argentina and Chile, on the Andean summit of Uspallata Pass.

The statue of Christ was made of bronze, after melting down the Argentinian cannons used against the Chileans, in a bitter conflict over their territorial boundaries. The inscription reads:

> Sooner shall these mountains crumble into dust than will Argentines and Chileans break the peace sworn at the feet of Christ the Redeemer.

After King Edward VII of Great Britain was asked to mediate the dispute between Argentina and Chile, the two governments signed a treaty ending the conflict in 1903. During the celebration that followed, Senora de Costa, a noble lady of Argentina, conceived the idea of the monument. At the dedication of the monument, "Christ of the Andes" was presented to the world, with the ringing prayer of Senora de Costa:

Protect, O Lord, our native land. Ever give us faith and hope. May fruitful peace be our first patrimony and good example its greatest glory.

The Prince of Peace

In view of such a story, one wonders how could Papal Christians, as prophesied at Daniel 7, verse 25, persecute Protestant Christians, as prophesied at Revelation 12, verse 6; thereby driving the saints of God into a wilderness experience. I submit, the reason is they were not drawn to Christ, the Prince of Peace, who taught, "Blessed are the peace makers: for they shall be called the children of God" (Matthew 5:9). Jesus also said, "And I, if I be lifted up from the earth, will draw all men unto me" (John 12:32). And to those who are in fact *drawn to Christ* He said, "Peace I leave with you, My peace I give unto you: not as the world give I unto you" (John 14:27). Those who possess that peace, will be those who overcome the devil "by the blood of the Lamb, and by the word of their testimony; and they loved not their lives unto the death" (Revelation 12:11).

(3)
RISE OF THE CHURCH AT ROME

Edict of Milan, A.D. 313

Going back to the beginning of the Christian era, the early Christian church emerged from the tenth and worst wave of persecution that lasted ten years, under the pagan Roman Emperor Diocletian. The signal for the end of persecution was the Edict of Milan, A.D. 313, promulgated by Constantine the Great. It was an edict of toleration of Christianity and other religions that changed the course of history. The text of the edict declared:

> the worship of God ought rightly to be our first and chiefest care, and that it was right that Christians and all others should have freedom to follow the kind of religion they favored.... Moreover, concerning the Christians, we before gave orders with respect to the places set apart for their worship. It is now our pleasure that all who have bought such places should restore them to the Christians, without any demand for payment.

Constantine the Great

The effect of the edict was that Christianity was made a *religio licita*—a legal religion, on a par with all other religions. While the edict hesitated to place Christianity above other religions of the empire, the return of houses of worship by the pagan religions tended to favor the Christians. The result was, that Constantine himself directed the building of the first church of Saint Peter, much to the chagrin and wrath of his non-Christian subjects. He also ordered the building of the church of the Holy Sepulchre above the very sights of the crucifixion and Jesus' tomb, by removing the Roman temple of Venus. Constantine's mother, Helena, directed the building of a few churches on sites venerated by Christians. Thus, the provisions of the edict led to a thriving period of reconstruction and building of churches, that resulted in an increasingly Christian empire.

What precipitated the Edict of Milan? It was the purported conversion of Constantine to Christianity. On the eve of the Battle of Milvian Bridge, it is reported that Constantine had a vision to enter the battle, trusting in the God of the Christians. He won the battle and took control of the Western empire in 312. By 324 Constantine became sole Roman emperor, besides being the first Christian emperor. (See Photo 8).

Photo 8

Arch of Constantine, Rome, Italy

The Arch was built to commemorate Constantine's victory in the battle of Milvian Bridge. Christianity gained a different victory through Constantine's Edict of Toleration, 313. But Christianity lost in the battle for Truth, when Constantine issued his Sunday Law, 321.

Constantine's Sunday Law, A.D. 321

Constantine's Christian leanings can be glimpsed in his legal enactments. Outstanding of which is the earliest Sunday law known to history in the year 321, as follows:

> On the venerable day of the sun let all the magistrates and people residing in the cities rest, and let all the workshops be closed. In the country, however, persons engaged in agriculture may freely and lawfully continue their pursuits.[1]

It will be noted that the "venerable day of the sun" refers to Sunday. Bishop Sylvester I of Rome, the contemporary of Constantine, decreed that Sunday should not be called the "day of the sun," but the Lord's Day.

Council of Laodicea Circa A.D. 364

What began as a pagan ordinance, ended as a Christian regulation. Close on the heels of the Sunday Edict of Constantine followed the Church Council of Laodicea (circa A.D. 364) that enjoined:

> Christians shall not Judaize and be idle on Saturday [Sabbath], but shall work on that day; but the Lord's day they shall especially honour, and, as being Christians, shall, if possible, do no work on that day. If, however, they are found Judaizing, they shall be shut out from Christ.[2]

Implicit in this strong worded ecclesiastical decree, is the fact that Christians within the Roman empire, were *observing* the Sabbath day which occurred on Saturday, the seventh day of the week. To observe the Sabbath of the Bible was stigmatized as Judaizing. Hence, the church dictated that the practice cease forthwith, and that the Lord's day, being Sunday, should be honored. To continue Sabbath observance, meant being anathematized—that is "they shall be shut out from Christ," tantamount to excommunication.

Such were the far-reaching developments after Constantine's Sunday law. There were others that had a profound effect on the church, as Constantine left his mold on the church, for example he told a group of bishops:

You are bishops whose jurisdiction is within the church; I also am a bishop, ordained by God to overlook those outside the church.[3]

Council of Nicaea A.D. 325

As a consequence of those words internal state matters became Christianized—a union of church and state was in the making. Constantine became involved in church matters. He convened and presided over the Church Council of Nicaea in 325 to define orthodox doctrine, and to check heresy, by he himself exiling Arius. Constantine thereby, formulated the pattern for the future, and Eusebius, contemporary church historian, constructed an extravagant theology of the Christian emperor, painting a picture of Constantine's glorious reign as:

One might have thought that a picture of Christ's kingdom was thus shadowed forth, and a dream rather than reality.[4]

Emperor Justinian

We have traced the effects of the legal recognition of Christianity in the rise of the church at Rome. We are also reminded of the aspirations of Pope Leo the Great, for legal recognition of Rome's headship over all the churches and dioceses. That did not come until the reign of Justinian, emperor of the Eastern Roman Empire seated in Constantinople, after Constantine split the Roman empire in two, back in the year 330.

Justinian I (527–565), not only guided the destinies of the Roman empire for thirty eight years, but also gave to the world the great *Corpus Juris Civilis*—Body of Civil Law. This Body of Civil Law also incorporated edicts of former emperors in favor of the Roman church, and the canons of former general Church Councils relating to faith, morals and discipline. Above all, it singled out the Bishop of Rome as the *legal* "*Head* of all the Holy Churches."

Justinian had uprooted the third heretical Arian kingdom of the Goths in 538, giving the *Papacy* free reign over Christendom. In the same year Justinian's *legal* recognition of the *Pope* at Rome really went into effect. Thus commenced Papal Supremacy for 1,260 years (according to Daniel 7, verse 25), as the Universal Head of the Church wielding power to enforce ecclesiastical decrees and civil penalties.

Papal States

Not satisfied with the ecclesiastical supremacy recognized by Justinian, the church at Rome sought for *temporal* dominion. This was occasioned by the Lombards, when they seized Ravenna, the imperial capital, ravaged Italy, and threatened Rome. Pope Stephen II sought the aid of Pepin, king of the Franks to restore the domain of St. Peter.

Pepin drove the Lombards back, and responded by restoring the domain of St. Peter, comprising a triangle of the east coast of Italy bordered by Bologna, Ravenna and Ancona. This resulted in the pope becoming a temporal ruler with the establishment in 755 of the Papal States.

"Donation of Constantine"

In order to bring about the acquisition of this papal domain as a restoration, Pope Stephen evidently presented to King Pepin an ancient document: the "Donation of Constantine," dated March 30, A.D. 315. It related, how Constantine on his determined departure for Constantinople, bequeathed to Peter, the first Vicar of the Son of God, and his successors the following gift:

> Lo! we give and grant, not only our palace as aforesaid, but also the city of Rome, and all the provinces and palaces and cities of Italy and of the western regions, to our aforesaid most blessed Pontiff and universal Pope.[5]

The "Donation of Constantine" was a very impressive document. It demonstrated the abdication of *pagan* Rome to Christian Rome. It proved that the pope was *successor* to Peter and Constantine. It granted territorial sovereignty to the successors of Saint Peter, enhancing the image of the pope on an equal footing, as one of the sovereign powers of Europe.

But, the "Donation of Constantine" was a forgery—the most famous in European history. It was not written in 315, but about half way through the eighth century, in time for Pope Stephen to use it. And successive popes like Leo IX and Urban II, appealed to it, and it continued to be influential, until Laurentius Valla proved it to be a forgery in 1440. But, in fear and trepidation of reprisals Valla's book was not published until 1517. That was also the critical year in which Luther attacked indulgences. Luther read Valla's book and concluded that his earlier faith in the papacy was based on forgeries. Rome also read Valla's book, yet continued for centuries to authenticate the Donation of Constantine. Only in 1789 did Pope Pius VI admit the Decretals a fraud.

Papal Sovereignty

A final word on the significance of Pope Stephen's visit with King Pepin. For the first time a pope sought military aid from a western king. There would be more to follow. Second, the restoration of the land by Pepin, whether it included the territory outlined in the Donation of Constantine or not, was a significant maneuver. It also played right into the hands of the prophecy of the "little horn" that was "different" from the other political horns (Remember Daniel 7:24). The papacy became a religio-political power different from its fellow political powers. Here was a spiritual sovereign, Universal Head of the Church, assuming temporal sovereignty over land—the Papal States. And that sovereignty was maintained and fought for, even up to the time of Luther, under the "warrior pope" Julian II. Sovereignty continued right up to the nineteenth century, when the papacy was divested of its Papal States, leaving it with a token state—the Vatican. But that is sufficient to give the papacy a political edge.

Charlemagne

Enter Charlemagne, son of Pepin, who like his father before him, endowed the church at Rome with more territory, and was rewarded by being crowned in the year 800, the first emperor of the Holy Roman Empire. That empire lasted until 1806, as already discussed in Chapter 1. As great Protector of the church, Charlemagne attempted a Christian theocracy on the Augustinian pattern—a virtual *Christendom*, with Charlemagne receiving the crown from papal hands, there occurs the possibility of withdrawing the crown. The withdrawing of the crown, suggests the desire for the papacy to assume supreme power and control over imperial power, and that introduces a new phase in the rise of the church at Rome.

We have discussed three emperors: Constantine, Justinian, and Charlemagne, virtual Protectors of the Church. We now consider three popes who propelled the Church at Rome to dizzy heights: Gregory VII (1073–1085), Innocent III (1198–1216), and Boniface VIII (1294–1303).

Pope Gregory VII

Pope Gregory VII, upon ascending the throne of Saint Peter, set about instituting three reforms: he decreed strict celibacy for the priests, and attacked simony, and lay investiture. The latter put him on a collision course with an emperor who refused to acquiesce. Pope Gregory promptly excommunicated King Henry IV of Germany, absolving his subjects of allegiance to him and declared, "Emperor Henry is deprived of his kingdom of Germany and Italy."

The Humiliation of Canossa (1077) as described in Chapter 1, brought about a reversal of the pope's anathema, after King Henry's penance. This was the first time a pope had deigned to depose a king. Such was the level of arrogance assumed by the papacy. And Gregory did it several times: he deposed the

Greek emperor and the Polish king. These acts brought about a baleful harvest of unrest and rebellion. Gregory set a trend and later popes excommunicated emperors and deposed some.

"Dictatus"

The power to depose emperors and kings, and to absolve their subjects from oaths of fidelity, was among the twenty seven propositions incorporated in Gregory's "Dictatus," spelled out when he became pope. Other pretentious claims are enumerated:

The pope alone can depose bishops and reinstate them; The pope is the only person whose feet are kissed by all emperors; The pope alone is entitled to imperial insignia; No one can be considered Catholic who does not agree with the Roman Church; The pope's decree can be annulled by no one, and that he alone may annul the decrees of any one; The Roman Church has never erred, nor ever by the testimony of Scripture shall err, to all eternity.

Among these claims, one of the most staggering is that the pope ought to judge all the world, and to be judged by none. It is ironic to claim that "the Roman church has never erred," which by the way is a claim of infallibility, because most of these propositions were based on error-forged documents, such as the pseudo-Isidorean decretals. This is what the Catholic theologian Dollinger had to say:

Without the pseudo-Isidore there would have been no Gregory VII.[6]

Pope Innocent III

If Gregory VII was the Julius Caesar of the papal empire, Pope Innocent III was the Augustus. If Gregory carried out the sentiments of "Dictatus," Innocent extended them to the limit. Under Innocent the peak of power was culminated, and the theocratic principle was established. Not satisfied that the whole church was entrusted to the successors of Saint Peter, Innocent strove for the whole world. To achieve these ends he employed the power of excommunication and Interdict, the Inquisition and Crusade.

Interdict

Soon after Innocent became pope he put France under an interdict for eight months. But, in 1208 he plunged England into chaos by means of an interdict for six years, in an endeavor to force King John to obedience. The severe measures of the interdict meant all cathedrals and churches were closed, the communion was withheld, nearly all religious rites were suspended—Christ was withdrawn. It practically stopped all civil government. In the next year King John was excommunicated. Three years later he was deposed. There seemed no way out.

Finally, King John capitulated and surrendered England itself, "to God and to our Lord Pope Innocent." He would receive England back under annual payment of rent as a vassal of the pope, and all religious rights would be restored—Christ was back in circulation. This situation prevailed until 1333, when King Edward III refused to pay the annual rent.

Innocent was not yet through with King John and England. When the "Magna Carta" was drawn up in 1215, guaranteeing the rights of man, Innocent condemned it, and excommunicated those who observed it.

Inquisition

The year 1215 marked another event, a religious one. Innocent convened the Fourth Lateran Council with about fifteen hundred in attendance. Two important decisions taken were the definition and canonization of the dogma of transubstantiation, and the canonization of the Inquisition. That meant systematizing the Inquisition by council action, and pronouncing it the "Holy Office." It was designed as a sacred activity to root out heresy, however minute that may be, in order to maintain the purity of the faith. The pope's Holy Office was the pope's spiritual spy system. The bishops were instructed to make the rounds of their dioceses, at least once a year, to search out heresy. They also had their informants to help them, and this set brother against brother. The inquisitorial system invaded the sanctity of the conscience. It was a tyranny over the souls of mankind. After its establishment it took on fearsome proportions. Innocent IV added torture. It brought agony to countless millions and the shedding of veritable streams of blood.

Crusade

So-called heresy had been around in Languedoc, southeastern France for a century. Dominic, founder of the Dominican Order, preached to the Albigenses to no avail. They were fully convinced that the medieval church was corrupt, befitting the Babylon of the Apocalypse, and that they could be saved outside of the church. Whereupon, Innocent III ordered a Crusade (1209) against the Albigensian heretics on a grand scale, comparable to the crusading zeal evinced against the Moslem infidels. 20,000 knights and 200,000 ruffian footmen were guaranteed the highest place in heaven, as they advanced with a scorched-earth policy and indiscriminate carnage. 20,000 were slaughtered in the first encounter at Beziers. The carnage continued until 1229, but not until hundreds of thousands were slaughtered. Then the Inquisition took over and by 1250 the Albigenses were well nigh exterminated. The slaughter of Christians by Innocent outstripped by far that of the Roman emperor Diocletian.

The Crusade of pope Innocent III was a landmark in the history of Christianity, one that truly belied the name Innocent. A landmark that belied the name of Christ, by doing exactly what Christ wouldn't do; what a DEPARTURE FROM CHRIST!

Pope Boniface VIII

Boniface VIII gave final shape and form to papal power by his most presumptuous claims and arrogance. These are well defined in his famous bull—"Unam Sanctam" issued 1302, quoted below:

> Urged on by our faith, we are obliged to believe and hold that there is only one holy, catholic, and apostolic church.... Outside of her there is no salvation nor remission of sins.
>
> Furthermore, that every human creature is subject to the Roman pontiff,—this we declare, say, define, and pronounce to be altogether necessary to salvation.[7]

I add no comments; as you read the above, you may ponder the implications. But, the following taken from "Unam Sanctam" may astound you, that in the church and within her power are two swords:

> Therefore, both are in the power of the church, namely, the spiritual sword and the temporal sword; the latter is to be used for the church, the former by the church.[8]

When the year 1300 had arrived, Boniface must have displayed a "bonny face," because he proclaimed it the Jubilee Year. About two million pilgrims visited Rome, endowing the church with heaps of gold and silver in exchange for indulgences. And on that jubilant note we conclude this story.

2 Thessalonians, Chapter 2

The heyday of papal supremacy over the church and the world having been enhanced by the aforementioned three popes, made thinking people wonder, whether it was the true church of Christ. It drove them to study their Bibles to find out. In fact, long before the medieval church had reached such stupendous heights, there were some that read the Bible with foreboding; none other than Augustine a champion of Christianity in search of truth. And Augustine read from 2 Thessalonians, chapter two:

> v. 1. Now concerning the coming of our Lord Jesus Christ, and our gathering together to Him, we ask you
>
> v. 2. not to be soon shaken in mind or troubled, either by spirit or by word or by letter, as if from us, as though the day of Christ had come.
>
> v. 3. Let no one deceive you by any means; for that Day will not come unless the falling away comes first, and that man of sin is revealed, the son of perdition,
>
> v. 4. who opposes and exalts himself above all that is called God or that is worshiped, so that he sits as God in the temple of God, showing himself that he is God.

v. 5. Do you not remember that when I was still with you I told you these things?

v. 6. And now you know what is restraining that he may be revealed in his own time.

v. 7. For the mystery of lawlessness is already at work; only He who now restrains will do so until he is taken out of the way.

v. 8. And then the lawless one will be revealed, whom the Lord will consume with the breath of His mouth and destroy with the brightness of His coming.

v. 9. The coming of the lawless one is according to the working of Satan, with all power, signs, and lying wonders,

v.10. And with all unrighteous deception among those who perish, because they did not receive the love of the truth, that they might be saved.

v.11. And for this reason God will send them strong delusion, that they should believe the lie,

v.12. that they all may be condemned who did not believe the truth but had pleasure in unrighteousness.

The New King James Version

Summary: 2 Thessalonians 2

In order to summarize 2 Thessalonians, chapter two, one needs to discover why the second epistle to the Thessalonian church was written. The emphasis of the first epistle is climaxed at 1 Thessalonians, chapter four, describing the all consuming event of the Second Coming of Christ. This had made such an impact on the minds of the Thessalonian Christians, that they thought Christ's Second Coming was imminent. Paul wanted to put their minds at ease, by writing to them the second epistle, showing that the Second Coming was not that imminent, since there was to be the development of an event, still to shape up before the Second Coming. Hence, "concerning the coming of our Lord Jesus Christ" do "not be soon shaken in mind," whether "by letter" (reference to the first epistle or letter), or whatever. "For that day"—referring to the Second Coming—"will not come unless the falling away comes first." The falling away is a specific fall away. The expression "falling away" translates the Greek "*apostasia*"—from which we get the word *apostasy*. The "falling away" or apostasy refers to the *church*. That is, the Christian church is going to fall into apostasy before the Second Coming of Christ.

With the falling away or apostasy of the Christian Church the "man of sin" is to be eventually revealed. The man of sin is equated with the "mystery of lawlessness" (verse 7), and the "*lawless one*" (verse 8,9). Paul was acquainted with the prophecy of Daniel, chapter seven. Could not the lawless one or mystery of lawlessness be equated with the "little horn" that "shall intend to change times and *law*" (Daniel 7:25)?

Rome: The Restraining Power

When will this specific fall away of the church and the mystery of lawlessness take place? The time of its revealing is of utmost importance. Paul says it would be "revealed in his own time" (verse 6). Paul says in the next verse that the time of revelation will occur when the power who now restrains the revelation, is "taken out of the way" (verse 7). Paul says the Thessalonian church knows what is restraining or preventing the appearance of the lawless one—"you know what is restraining that he may be revealed" (verse 6). Paul did not identify the *restraining power* which they knew to be Rome, for fear of reprisals. Remember the Christian church was under persecution by Rome. If the Thessalonian Christians were aware of Daniel seven, showing the rise of the "little horn" after the fourth kingdom of Rome (See Daniel 7:8,24), then the *restraining power of Rome* against the revelation of the *Great Apostasy* of the Christian Church made sense.

Paul told the Thessalonians that the mystery of lawlessness was in fact "already at work"—hidden that is, until the restraining power of Rome "is taken out of the way" (verse 7).

How will the Apostasy arise? Paul says "the coming of the lawless one is according to the working of Satan, with all power, signs and lying wonders" (verse 9)—watch for them!

What are the characteristics of the Apostasy or lawless one? "Who opposes and exalts himself above all that is called God or that is worshipped, so that he sits as God in the temple of God, showing himself that he is God" (verse 4). Were the Thessalonians aware that the "little horn" of Daniel seven had similar characteristics: "He shall speak pompous words against the Most High" (Daniel 7:25). Then what Paul told them made sense.

Augustine's Exposition

Augustine read Paul's message to the Thessalonians and it also made sense to him as he explained the *Roman Empire as the restraining power*:

> Some think that the Apostle Paul referred to the Roman empire, and that he was unwilling to use language more explicit, lest he should incur the calumnious charge of wishing ill to the empire which it is hoped would be eternal.... However, it is not absurd to believe that these words of the apostle, 'Only he who now holdeth, let him hold until he be taken out of the way,' refer to the Roman empire.... 'And then shall that wicked be revealed': no one doubts that means Antichrist.[9]

Apostasy in The Church

Although Augustine sets forth different views, he inclines toward the Apostasy or lawless one appearing as an apostate body in the *Christian Church*. Here is Augustine's exposition:

> This day should not come unless he first came who is called the apostate—apostate, to wit, from the Lord God....
>
> But it is uncertain in what temple he shall sit, whether in that ruin of the temple which was built by Solomon, or in the church; for the apostle would not call the temple of any idol or demon the temple of God. And on this account some think that in this passage Antichrist means not the prince himself alone, but his whole body, that is, the mass of men who adhere to him, along with him their prince; and they also think that we should render the Greek more exactly were we to read, not 'in the temple of God,' but 'for' or 'as the temple of God,' as if he himself were the temple of God, the Church.[10]

Thank God that Augustine this time applied the simple, sober grammatico-historical interpretation to Paul's prophecy, and arrived at truth. On this subject he was in good company with his fellow Greek church father John Chrysostom who expressed similar understanding. Likewise, he was in good company with the great Jerome, who produced the Latin Vulgate Bible. Jerome stated his interpretation without wavering as follows:

> And [Antichrist] may sit in the temple of God, either Jerusalem (as some think) or in the church (as we more truly think), showing himself as if he himself were Christ, and the Son of God.[11]

The points that stand out in bold relief about Paul's prophecy are:

(1) A falling away or Apostasy (as Chrysostom said) of the church is to be revealed gradually *after* the fall of Rome;

(2) the apostasy will sit in the temple of God, the *church*;

(3) the Apostasy takes place before the Second Coming of Christ and continues until destroyed "with the brightness of His coming" (verse 8).

Stealthy Rise of Apostasy

We are grateful for the clear-cut exposition of Paul's prophecy given by these early expositors of the fifth century. But none of them saw the fulfillment of the prophecy. And those that followed, down through the centuries, took some time to detect the Apostasy, because its true colors were not fully revealed, since it advanced subtly, stealthily with "all power, signs and lying wonders." Furthermore, because people "did not receive the love of the truth," they were inclined to "believe the lie" (verse 10,11).

Nevertheless, as the year A.D. 1000 approached, agitation of soul made people think the end of the world was imminent—the church divines, however, were unmoved. The millennial year passed without any upheaval. But, the passing of the twelfth century gave expositors the opportunity for interpreting the 1,260 days of Revelation twelve, verse six, and related time periods to mean 1,260 years. Hence the year A.D. 1260 suggested itself, as a terminus for the end of the world.

Joachim

From this setting emerged a new spiritual awakening under Joachim (1130–1202) and a new interpretation of prophecy. Joachim, the abbot and scholar from Floris, Calabria, located in the instep of the boot of Italy, was hailed a keen theologian by Dollinger. Dante said Joachim was "endowed with prophetic spirit," but Joachim never made that claim, instead he felt a special call came to him as an expositor of prophecy.

Joachim's prophetic writings were not condemned by the Fourth Lateran Council convened by Innocent III. After Joachim's death his prophetic writings either influenced, or won the admiration of the two orders founded by Saint Francis and Saint Dominic, the Spiritual Franciscans, Wycliffe and the Lollards, Cardinal Cusa, Huss, the French reformer George Pacard, and the German reformer Andreas Osiander. Joachim's two principal books were printed in Venice in 1519 and 1527 respectively.

As Joachim was DRAWN TO CHRIST, he lived a humble Christian life, that foreshadowed the awakening of an evangelical age within the confines of the medieval church, that he named the Age of the Spirit. The sole aim of the age was to imitate Christ—*Imitatio Christi*. Such an age continued to develop and was epitomized in Francis of Assissi. Many started out in imitation of Christ as mendicant friars. This age caught fire in Italy, southern France, northeastern Spain, and England.

The effect of the age that Joachim set in motion, was averse to the hierarchy, bent on power, prestige and wealth. The introduction of this age ran counter to the Augustinian principle related in the "City of God." The pure evangelical morals of the age would tend to become a standard by which to judge and criticize the papal hierarchy, to consider it the Great Apostasy.

Joachim, it is reputed, told Richard I, the Lionhearted king of England, that the Antichrist was already born in the city of Rome, and would be elevated to the papal throne. On another occasion Joachim wrote:

> Antichrist will usurp for himself the kingdom of Christ, saying that he is the Son of God, and he will sit as Lord in His temple, seeking to extinguish the Vicar of Christ.... [12]

Joachim's new interpretation of prophecy dealt a blow to the Tichonius—Augustine View. This view applied all the elements of the millennium of

Revelation twenty, to the Christian church from a spiritual point of view, rather than a prophetic point of view. Augustine's view was also a non-historical approach to the book of Revelation, setting forth abstract principles to the church with little regard to prophecy, or to time and place. The progressive unveiling of prophecy was not considered historical in fulfillment. The chronological fulfillment of events was lost sight of. And this Tichonius—Augustinian tradition prevailed for seven centuries (See Appendix A). It was a denial of the principle enunciated by Jesus, "I have told you before it come to pass, that when it is come to pass, ye might believe" (John 14:29).

Jesus' Principle of Prophetic Interpretation

Joachim restored Jesus' principle, that prophecy unfolds progressively; it comes to pass in time—historic time. Having laid the foundation of the historical age of the Old Testament and the New Testament, Joachim finds an historical base for the *septimal figures* of Revelation: the 7 Seals (Revelation 6:1 to 8:1); the 7 Trumpets (Revelation 8:2 to 10:7); the 7 Vials or Plagues (Revelation 15,16). Each of the septimal figures run parallel through seven eventful chronological periods, from the time of Christ to the great consummation—being a period of 1,260 years.

Into the Apocalyptic scheme of 1,260 years Joachim placed the Two Witnesses (Revelation 11), the Sun-clothed Woman (Revelation 12) and the Beast (Revelation 13). Of course, the latter *three figures* fit into the 1,260 year scheme because their respective contexts suggest the time period as 1,260 days, 42 months, 3½ times or prophetic years (being 3½ x 360 prophetic days = 1,260 days). The Apocalyptic scheme concludes with the destruction of Antichrist and the commencement of the millennium of Revelation twenty (Please See Appendix B for a clear picture).

Consummation of the Ages

From Joachim's perspective he figured the consummation of the ages would occur around the year 1260. From our perspective in the twentieth century, we know that was not true. But, his *placement of the prophetic figures* in his Apocalyptic scheme, with some fine tuning and minor changes, is today theologically sound. This was a historic breakthrough, and his scheme is still within the entire Christian era, the terminus of which is not the year 1260, but beyond. The terminus is not given in Scripture. It is not the twentieth century, and is therefore not known.

Again, the 1,260 year period (stated at Revelation 11:2,3; 12:6,14; 13:5) stipulated for the sun-clothed church in the wilderness has been placed to start from the year 538, a date from Joachim's perspective, unknown. Nevertheless, before the year 1200, the light of truth burst into his mind, and that moment of truth was expressed in these words:

> The woman clothed with the sun, who signifies the church, remained hidden in the wilderness from the face of the serpent, a day without doubt being accepted for a year, and a thousand two hundred and sixty days for the same number of years.[13]

Joachim Discovers Day-Year Principle

Although Joachim was the first Christian expositor to apply the *day for a year principle* to prophetic time periods, Jewish expositors had applied it since Nahawendi in the early ninth century. Why wasn't it applied earlier still, like in the fifth century?

Inspiration couched the expression 1,260 days or 3½ times (a time, times, and half a time at Revelation 12:6,14) in cryptic language, so as not to discourage men like Jerome and Augustine of the fifth century. They interpreted the existence of the Antichrist to be 1260 literal days or 3½ literal years, in order that the Second Coming of Jesus would not be delayed. It would be discouragement for them to wait at least another 1,260 literal years before Jesus returned. Perhaps, that is why Paul never introduced a specific time frame for the Great Apostasy, when addressing the Thessalonians who were also looking for an imminent Second Coming.

On the other hand, from our perspective, knowing that the great apostasy was to commence, when the restraining power of Rome was removed, it would be ridiculous to apply 1,260 literal days, equal to a mere 3 ½ year period, followed by the Second Coming. That would mean, the apostasy would have ended in the sixth century after 538. However, it is more plausible to add 1,260 literal years to 538 reaching down to 1798, for the existence of the papal little horn, or apostasy. Then to be followed much later by the consummation of the Second Coming.

Apart from the cryptic language of Inspiration, it appears that the Holy Spirit drew His hand over the 1,260 day prophecy, until Joachim discovered its meaning. Strange, that Augustine employed the day-year principle for the "70 weeks" of years (70 x 7 days per week = 490 days-years), apportioned to the Jewish nation recorded in Daniel, chapter nine, verse 24. But, Augustine was oblivious to applying the day-year principle to the 1,260 days.

Archbishop Eberhard II Identifies Papal Little Horn

While Joachim was the first Christian expositor to apply the truth of the day-year principle, and lay out a purely historical scheme of fulfilling prophecy, Archbishop Eberhard II of Salzburg, Germany,(A.D. 1240), was the first to apply the "little horn" of Daniel, chapter seven, to the Historical Papacy. Remember, in chapter two we viewed the monument in Nuremberg, depicting the Drama of the Apocalyptical Beasts of Daniel seven, and discussed the interpretation of the reformer, Osiander.

The creation of the Holy Roman Empire tended to blunten the fact, that Rome collapsed, and was divided into ten divisions. Eberhard was not blinded by this notion, that had also been fueled by Augustinianism. He laid the truth bare, showing that the "little horn" would arise "among" and "after" the ten divisions, uprooting three horn entities (Daniel 7:8,24).

Since the Papacy had shown its true colors, that is "the lawless one will be revealed" (2 Thessalonians 2:8), Eberhard laid the ax to the tree, charging that Pope Gregory VII: "first laid the foundations of the empire of Antichrist." Eberhard bore in mind the characteristics of the "little horn" at Daniel seven, verse 25:

> He shall speak pompous words against the Most High,
> Shall persecute the saints of the Most High,
> And shall intend to change times and law.

The New King James Version

Armed with the characteristics of the "little horn," Eberhard applied them to the Papacy and they fitted like a glove. Eberhard recalled the pontificates of Gregory VII and Innocent III, bearing in mind the pretentious claims of "Dictatus" and their fulminations, Interdicts, Inquisition and Crusades—their cup of iniquity and lawlessness was full. Allusions to these claims and activities, matching Daniel's description and Paul's Apostasy, come through as clear as crystal in the epochal words of Eberhard, some portions of which are in italics:

> Those priests of Babylon alone desire to reign, they cannot tolerate an equal, they will not desist until they have trampled all things under their feet, and until they *sit in the temple of God*, and until they are *exalted above all that is worshipped*.... He who is servant of servants, desires to be lord of lords, just as if he were God.... He *speaks great things* as if he were truly God. He ponders new counsels under his breast, in order that he may establish his own rule for himself, he *changes laws*, he *ordains* his own laws, he *corrupts*, he *plunders*, he pillages, he defrauds, he *kills*—that incorrigible man (whom they are accustomed to call Antichrist) on whose forehead an inscription of insult is written: 'I am God, *I cannot err*.' He sits in the temple of God, and has dominion far and wide. But as it is in the secrets of the holy writings, let him that readeth understand.[14]

(Italics supplied)

Eberhard made no bones about fully identifying the Great Apostasy or "lawless one" related by Paul, including the "little horn" related by Daniel. He hit the nail square on the head of the Papacy, using the term Antichrist—whom others of his day were "accustomed" to use. He certainly was not rewarded for his significant identification—in fact he was excommunicated. And the Papacy shrugged its shoulders, and went on its determined way until startled by the Protestant Reformation—to be taken up later in this book.

Conclusion

Having arrived at this point in the Drama of the Ages we look back at what has happened. We have traced the rise of the church at Rome, only to find that by the thirteenth century, *voices within* the confines of the medieval Roman church, had shown that the church had fallen into Apostasy, and was therefore, not the true historic church of the apostolic succession. But, that does not mean that the hosts of Christians that came under the church's jurisdiction are lost. Salvation is a personal experience, and countless numbers of souls, who might have belonged to the church at Rome, will be saved, *irrespective* of the church.

If the church at Rome was not the true church, was there a true church, visible or invisible, that appeared on the horizon of history? The Drama of the Ages is not complete without such an investigation. We shall trace the existence of the true church in the next chapter.

(4)

RISE OF THE CHURCH IN THE WILDERNESS

To gain perspective for this chapter I take you back to Saint Peter's in Rome. We view again the Altar of the Chair depicting the four doctors—fathers of the Roman church supporting the throne of Saint Peter. In reality they supported and contributed to the elevation of the papacy.

Bishop Ambrose of Northern Italy (d.397)

Much space has been given to Augustine and his contribution regarding the rise of papal Rome. His companion, Latin church father Ambrose, whose preaching converted Augustine, will now be considered. While Ambrose is placed among that noble quartet of church fathers supporting the edifice of the papacy, he did in fact go out on a limb, supporting his archdiocese of northern Italy, independent of Rome, and never accepted the primacy of the bishop of Rome. Ambrose himself became bishop by acclamation, and the bishops of this diocese never went to Rome for ordination. Ambrose exercised great authority, rivaling that of the bishop of Rome.

Apart from an administrative independence from Rome, the archdiocese of northern Italy, of which Milan was the capital, practiced an independent ritual—the Ambrosian Liturgy. Ambrose himself did not acknowledge any authority on earth as superior to that of the Bible. Christ was the foundation of the church. He declared that nobody could pretend to call himself the successor of Saint Peter, unless he had the faith of St. Peter—in essence apostolic succession, rather than papal succession.

Although Ambrose sometimes resorted to the allegorical method of interpretation, he did advocate the Bible was its own expositor, and that the Christian could arrive at truth by comparing Scripture with Scripture, relative to the same subject. On the matter of doctrine Ambrose was somewhat enigmatic, but I believe he was DRAWN TO CHRIST, in that he taught the believer is justified only by the merits of Christ, through His expiatory sacrifice on the cross. Salvation by faith was defined as a vital personal contact with Christ, with remission of sins, not by any human merit from our works. The sacraments confer no grace of themselves, they are only the visible sign of that which we receive from the Savior. Of the so-called seven sacraments, Ambrose believed in two—Baptism and the Lord's Supper (which he administered under both kinds). The evangelical doctrines of Ambrose continued long after his death in the year 397, after he had occupied the bishop's seat for twenty three years. As a champion of Christianity in search of truth, Ambrose definitely took a path to truth, unlike Rome, and cut a path toward evangelicalism.

Milan, Rival of Rome

Milan, the seat of the archdiocese of northern Italy became a Christian city, it is claimed, before Rome. Remember, it was agreed at Milan to publish Constantine's famous Edict of Toleration in 313. Milan, situated in the plain at the foot of the Alps, commanded the gateway to the north and west of Italy, among the ten greatest cities of Europe.

As Rome spread out, the independence of Milan was a thorn in Rome's flesh—more especially aggravated by proximity with Rome, in the very land where the papacy had its seat. Then on top of it all, the archdiocese of Milan was extensive, including part of Lombardy and the Piedmont of northern Italy, stretching west to Dauphine in France, and in between were the valleys of the Cottian Alps—a citadel fashioned by Providence.

Cottian Alps of Northern Italy

The Cottian Alps was to become the greatest aggravation to Rome, because it was an ideal place nestled in the mountains, in the "wilderness." Such a situation was conducive to the study of the great truths of the Word of God, independent of Rome.

Vigilantius of Lyons, France, had a controversy with Jerome. But in 406 his controversy was extended by a treatise against superstitions, and the veneration of martyr's relics. But, the significance of the controversy, is that Vigilantius wrote from a place described by Jerome somewhere "between the Adriatic and the Alps of King Cotius."

The Cottian Alps presents a further extension of the ecclesiastical independence of the Milan archdiocese. I cite the incident, when Ambrose addressed the clergy of his diocese, complaining that some priests in the secluded areas of his diocese were against the enforcement of celibacy. Jovinian had taught that no additional merit could be obtained by celibacy. No doubt the followers of Jovinian, who were expelled from Milan by Ambrose, found asylum in the outlying secluded valleys of the Cottian Alps.

The independent spirit of northern Italy was again in evidence, when in the year 590, nine bishops solemnly renewed the protestation of their independence of the church at Rome.

Bishop of the Valleys: Claudius of Turin

The mantle of Ambrose and Vigilantius descended upon Claudius (died 839), bishop of Turin, northern Italy, comprising the Piedmont, with its plains, and mountainous valleys to the west including the Cottian Alps, that earned for him the title: "Bishop of the Valleys." In the tradition of his ancestors, Claudius maintained independence from Rome, gaining the title "Protestant of the ninth century.' As a Protestant then, he asserted the equality of all the apostles with Saint Peter, and that the church was not founded on Saint Peter or the pope, but Jesus Christ was the sole Head of the church. On the matter of salvation he attached no value to pretended meritorious works, and acknowledged faith alone in securing salvation. Therefore, he admonished that there was no need to run to Rome for pardon of sin. He ascribed no power to prayers made for the dead, and could not relish relic worship. He maintained the symbolical character of the Lord's Supper.

Claudius was well versed in the Scriptures which was his constant study, and from his pen came forth books and commentaries on Genesis, Exodus, Leviticus, Matthew, Ephesians and none other, than Galatians. His sole authority was the Scriptures—*sola scriptura*, and human tradition was repudiated. It's no wonder that his influence spread all over Italy, France, and Germany.

Claudius inveighed against the invocation of saints, and against kissing the cross in these words: "God commands to bear the cross, not to worship it; they wish to worship it because they are unwilling to bear it either spiritually or corporeally." Above all he opposed with great energy the worship of images, which he, like his predecessors, regarded as absolute idolatry—declaring image worship a clear violation of the second commandment. Claudius was joined by his contemporary on the other side of the Alps, Agobardus, archbishop of Lyons, in these protests against image worship.

The torch of truth kept ablaze by Ambrose, Vigilantius, and Claudius was soon to dim for a time in greater Piedmont, but in the seclusion of the Cottian Alps, was an ancient church that came to be known as Waldenses, who were holding high the torch of truth. Rorenco, prior of Saint Roch at Turin about 1630, filed this report on the origin and teachings of the Waldenses:

> They were not a new sect in the ninth and tenth centuries, and that Claude of Turin must have detached them from the church in the ninth century.[1]

The curtain did close down on the independence of the Milan diocese by the eleventh century, when the popes succeeded in establishing authority, under protest. But, despite the tightening papal control, northern Italy maintained an independent spirit, and evangelical truth became strong again in the thirteenth century. Nevertheless, in the wake of the papal takeover in the eleventh century, some protesters fled across the Alps and descended to the Rhine and the diocese of Cologne. Still others headed for the Alps of Piedmont and there maintained their evangelical faith and ancient independence.

Church in the Wilderness: Waldenses

We now turn our attention to the ancient church of the Waldenses that flourished for over a thousand years—the spiritual Israel of the Alps. They maintained the faith of Ambrose, Vigilantius, and Claudius, and all constituted together the "church in the wilderness" (Revelation 12:6).

The Italian Waldenses, also called the Vaudois, rendered that way, meaning *valleys*, inhabited the *Cottian Alps*. They shared their origin with the history of the archdiocese of northern Italy, from the fourth to the ninth century, as outlined in the foregoing pages.

Besides sharing such a history owing to their proximity with the archdiocese of northern Italy, the Vaudois obviously shared their evangelical faith—caught from Ambrose, Jovinian, Vigilantius, and Claudius. In later centuries an examination of their faith reveals this factor. They maintained a strong Biblicism and the absolute authority of the Bible. They denied the supremacy of Rome, rejected image worship, and taught the pure gospel.

Even if the Vaudois had no contact whatsoever with the archdiocese of northern Italy, was it not likely that the seeds of truth would have been scattered broadcast over all Italy during the pagan Roman persecutions? Would not Christians head for the Alpine valleys to escape persecution, just like Christians headed for the mountains at the Roman siege of Jerusalem?

Furthermore, the Alpine valleys are quite habitable, and in the days of Cotius, a great well-paved Roman road was constructed over Mount Genevre, or the Cottian Alps. The road extended from Milan to the sea at Boulogne, with branches to Spain and toward Britain. Where the road crossed the Alps it afforded easy access to any part of the Alpine valleys. Thus, the Cottian Alps would not deter Christians from finding refuge there, or from dwelling there, and taking the pure gospel with them.

High Antiquity of Italian Waldenses

Many sources may be cited for the origin and high antiquity of the Italian Waldenses. But, here is one from among their persecutors. Peter the Inquisitor described the Waldenses of Austria in 1398:

> They believe themselves the vicars and legitimate successors of the Apostles of Christ.[2]

Henri Arnoud, who led the "glorious return" of the refugee Waldenses back to their Alpine valleys in 1689, after wholesale persecution, following the Revocation of the Edict of Nantes, had this to say about Waldensian origin:

> The Vaudois are, in fact, descended from those refugees from Italy who, after St. Paul had there preached the gospel, abandoned their beautiful country and fled, like the woman mentioned in the Apocalypse, to these wild mountains, where they have to this day handed down the gospel from father to son in the same purity and simplicity as it was preached by St. Paul.[3]

Arnoud also paraphrases an early report made by the Inquisitor Reineri to the pope, that the Waldenses "have existed from time immemorial."[4]

On the occasion of the Waldenses declaring their solidarity with the Protestants, negotiated by the Reformer Farel and the Waldensian leader Morel at Chamforans (1532), Morel addressed the Protestants: "In all things however, we agree with you, and always from the time of the Apostles we have, thinking as you do, been in harmony concerning the faith."[5]

Chamforans was followed up by the Waldensian gift of the entire Bible in French to the Protestant Reformation (1535). Olivetan, cousin to Calvin, did the translation into French and wrote this tribute to the Waldenses: "they have always had the full enjoyment of that heavenly Truth contained in the Holy Scriptures, ever since they were enriched with the same by the Apostles themselves."[6]

Such are the testimonies of friends and foes on the origin and apostolic succession of the Waldenses. But did the Waldenses actually make that claim themselves?

Apostolic Succession

We examine the oldest extant document of the Waldenses from the twelfth century, entitled the "Noble Lesson," manuscript copies of which are today at Cambridge, Dublin, Geneva, and Grenoble. The Noble Lesson takes the form of an anonymous poem of 479 lines, copies of which must have been circulated. Evidently circulated for reading in church assembly—one way of keeping the Old and New Testament truths alive before the people. It was the equivalent of a confession of faith, and of evangelical heritage passed down from generation to generation. And without trying to push a point, or to prove anything, the claim of apostolic succession, obviously *spiritual*, rather than visible reads:

Now after the Apostles, were certain teachers, who taught the way of Jesus Christ our Saviour. And these are found even at this present day, But they are known to very few, who have a great desire to teach the way of Jesus Christ.[7]

Did not Ambrose contend that nobody could be a successor of Saint Peter, unless he had the *faith* of Saint Peter. Apostolic succession does not rest upon the transmission of ecclesiastical authority, but upon the transmission of a life actuated by faith, belief and truth as taught by the Apostles.

Two Historic Churches in Italy

We are, therefore, confronted with two historic churches in close proximity in Italy: the church at Rome, and the church of the valleys, the Vaudois—Waldenses. Both claim apostolic succession. But, the reality of the matter is:

(1) The Roman church was founded on Saint Peter and papal successors. The Vaudois was founded upon Christ.

(2) The Roman church was the result of papal succession. The Vaudois was the result of apostolic succession.

(3) The Roman church was militant with the sword of the Crusades in hand. The Vaudois was pacifist, the "sandaled ones," with the Bible in hand.

(4) The Roman church made its way to the Lateran basilica in magnificent procession. The Vaudois made their way to some Lombard farmhouse in secret.

(5) The Roman church has a priesthood. The Vaudois was a priesthood of believers.

(6) The Roman priest at confession says "*Ego te absolvo*—I absolve you of your sins." The Vaudois preacher at confession says: "God absolves you of your sins."

(7) For the Roman church dependence on, and obedience to the sacraments was the binding cord. The Vaudois were bound by the Holy Scriptures, and heresy or error was to be corrected by admonition, never by force or extreme compulsion and torture.

Waldensian Vernacular Scriptures

To continue the contrasts of the two historic churches. The Roman church authorized the Latin Vulgate version of the Bible as the only true and authentic version. The Waldenses produced the first known vernacular version of the New Testament in the twelfth century, which the Roman church considered vulgar, since it was in the "vulgar tongue." Almost immediately James I, king of Aragon and count of Provence prohibited circulation of the Holy Scriptures in the vernacular in 1213.

Despite papal anathema and the Inquisitor, Waldenses circulated their vernacular version among the common people. Written in minuscule, plain hand writing, these small portable volumes of the Holy Scriptures were ideally fitted for concealment, and found a ready response from the people. On the other hand, the ponderous folios of the Latin Vulgate, penned in characters of gold and silver, ornately decorated with gems, invited admiration, rather than study, and were not readily available.

Talking about Bibles, the Waldensian vernacular version preserved in some of their manuscripts the "Epistle to the Laodiceans," which is not found in the regular Protestant Bible. This inclusion is an added testimony to the antiquity of the Waldenses, since it leads us back to the fourth century.[8]

Waldensian Belief

So much for the Bibles, but what Bible truths did the Waldenses advocate? They generally held the following cardinal doctrines: the absolute authority and inspiration of the Holy Scriptures; the trinity of the Godhead; the sinful state of man; free salvation by Jesus Christ; and above all faith working by love. Here is an important footnote to the last mentioned tenet of faith:

> It is impossible for any in this life to fulfill the commandments of God if they have not faith; and they cannot love Him perfectly, nor with a proper love, if they keep not his commandments.[9]

The above statement reflects what Jesus said at John 14, verse 15: "If ye love me keep my commandments." These statements were taken seriously by the Waldenses. They rejected the worship of images of the saints, or their relics, including the veneration of the cross, as outright idolatry, forbidden by the second commandment. Likewise, they observed Sunday because it was enjoined by the fourth commandment. But, there were those classed as Waldenses in the broader sense: the Passagii and some among the "Waldensian Brethren," or Picards, of Bohemia, who took the fourth commandment quite literally, and observed the seventh day of the week—Saturday.[10]

There were some Waldensian merchants, who committed the Bible to memory, and often went on their way from Switzerland into Suabia, Bavaria and northern Italy. They refused to honor images, and had an aversion to relics. They lived on vegetables, rarely ate meat, and some of them never.[11] This, however, was not a general practice among Waldenses of the early twelfth century.

Peter Waldo

We now consider the Waldenses of the twelfth century from another point of view, and that is, that Peter Waldo, champion of Christianity in search of truth, enters the picture. And he is declared by some to be the founder of the Waldenses, and that certainly appears to be the case, judging from the similarity of his name with the Waldenses. But, although the name Waldo has come down to us, he himself went by the name Valdesius (Latin) when he made his profession of faith in 1180. His followers called him Valdes.[12]

To better understand Peter Waldo's connection with the Waldenses, we need to tell his amazing story of how he was DRAWN TO CHRIST, and truly became an imitator of Christ—*imitatio Christi*. Peter Waldo, a prosperous merchant of Lyons, France, had an experience similar to Martin Luther, who withdrew from the world, and entered a monastery after a fearful stroke of lightning. In the case of Waldo's conversion, the sudden death of a friend in a public gathering before his very eyes, drove him eventually to enquire of salvation.

The advice given Waldo, was that given by Christ to the rich young ruler, "If thou wilt be perfect go and sell that thou hast, and give to the poor, and thou shalt have treasure in heaven: and come and follow me" (Matthew 19:21). Waldo felt as though God spoke directly to him, and like Saint Francis later, he forsook the world, made provision for his wife, provided for his daughters in a nunnery, distributed his wealth among the poor, procured a translation of the Holy Scriptures, and took to the streets, preaching repentance, from about 1173. Such a phenomenal turn around, inspired a following to be known as the Poor Men of Lyons.

The preaching of the Word and its distribution by Waldo and his followers, did not wash with the Archbishop of Lyons. He forbade unauthorized preaching and evangelism. Waldo retorted that it is better "to obey God rather than men" (Acts 5:29). Next Waldo went to Rome to seek the sanction of the Pope Alexander III. Waldo presented no heresy—he expected the pope would give him his paternal blessing. Instead, he was in for a shock. The pope at the Lateran Council, 1179, applauded Waldo's devotion to poverty, but not the unauthorized preaching. You see, to authorize Waldo's preaching, would undermine the leadership of the Roman clergy, and as one of their number said, "they will end by turning all of us out."[13]

Besides, the Roman church wanted implicit obedience to the pope and the sacraments, rather than to Christ and the Holy Scriptures, that Waldo was circulating. Therefore, Waldo and his followers continued to preach, without authorization, and soon, like Luther, Waldo found that Scripture circulation, and pure gospel-preaching was what Rome could not endure.

The Roman church could not endure Waldo any longer, so the final blow to his ministry came in 1184. Waldo and the Poor Men of Lyons were excommunicated, and exiled by the Archbishop of Lyons. Persecution set in. Waldo took refuge in Dauphine for a while, then retreated to Belgium and Picardy, and from thence to Germany. Eventually Waldo settled in Bohemia where he died about 1206.

Waldo's example of preaching and circulating the Scriptures was vigorously prosecuted in southern France. Likewise in Piedmont and Lombardy, of northern Italy, where they mingled with the older sects of the Vaudois and Poor of Lombardy; thereby enriching and embracing them, to constitute the Waldenses in a broader sense.

Fusion of French and Italian Waldenses

While the Fourth Lateran Council, 1215, under Innocent III, was designed to tighten authority and centralize power, evangelical Christians were preparing their agenda for a meeting in Bergamo, Italy, 1218, that would spark anew the Waldensian movement. The council of twelve, comprising six representatives each, from the Poor of Lyons and the Poor of Lombardy, declared their solidarity. Conscious that they were living in the last days, they were fired with an urgency to fulfill the apostolic mission. Thus, the French Waldenses, followers of their *founder* Peter Waldo, were united or fused with the *older* Italian Waldenses—the Vaudois Christians of the Alpine valleys.

Italian Waldenses: Anterior to Peter Waldo

Did I say *older* Italian Waldenses? Yes! We have already established the high antiquity of the Italian Waldenses, but here is more. Even while commenting on the Poor Men of Lyons, Burchard of Ursperg, had to chronicle in 1212 that the Leonists had long since sprung up in Italy.[14]

Since the Vaudois, never did designate any name for themselves, it is difficult to trace their existence by name, except that they would be seen as *separated or heretical* by their adversaries. Therefore, after the bishopric of Claudius, Bishop Hatto who held the diocese of Vercelli in 945 between Turin and Milan, wrote to the faithful of his diocese that, "there are many among you who have *separated* themselves from our holy mother church."[15] Likewise, writing somewhere between 1108 and 1136, Abbot Rodolph was anxious about crossing a country in the *Alps* on his way to Rome, that was "polluted with an inveterate heresy."[16]

Armed with a smattering of Latin we can easily determine, that the Vaudois or Italian Waldenses were also designated by the name Waldenses, other than the followers of Waldo. Another etymology of the name Vaudois is contained in the Latin words: Vallenses from *vallis*, a valley; and Valdenses from *vallis* + *densa*, a shady or dense valley. Therefore, Eberhard of Bethune, 1212, makes no mention of Waldo as founder and says: "Certain heretics call themselves *VALLENSES*, because they dwell in a vale of sorrow or tears." Likewise, Bernard, Abbot of Fontcaud, writing about 1190, alluding to events prior to the death of Pope Lucius II, 1144, described the Vaudois: "While Pope Lucius, of glorious memory, presided over the Holy Roman Church, new heretics suddenly raised their heads, who received a name that was an omen of their future lot, being called VALDENSES, from a dark dense valley, because they are involved in deep and thick shades."[17]

"Noble Lesson": Anterior to Peter Waldo

The oldest extant document of the Waldenses from the late twelfth century, namely the "Noble Lesson," has a *strong Italian flavor* derived from the influence of the Italian Joachim, the details of which are difficult to express in the running text of this chapter.[18] It is even claimed that the teachings of the Noble Lesson are a continuation of Claudius of Turin.[19] Second, but most significant, is that the Noble Lesson was composed in the local *Romaunt dialect*, or patois, of the Piedmont Alps, and not of the Lyonnais.[20] This factor establishes the *earlier settled existence* of the Vaudois or Italian Waldenses, by the time the French Waldenses came into existence under the leadership of Waldo of Lyons.

It has been necessary to trace and establish the history of the Italian branch of the Waldenses, because there has been a concerted attempt by Roman Catholics and Protestants to discredit the lineal descent of the Italian Waldenses, in favor of the origin of the Waldenses only in the twelfth century, founded by Peter Waldo. Such a contention, still fostered today, unfortunately, would leave the Roman church, as the one and only true historic church of all ages, and that would mean the arising of the Waldenses and the Protestants would be mere heretical novelties. Hence, the role of Waldo, who may be credited with founding the French Waldenses, facilitated a fusion of the French and older Italian Waldenses, including all their evangelical forerunners, into a grand Waldensian movement.

Remember, that in the beginning of this chapter we traced the *true historic church* of northern Italy, through Ambrose, Jovinian, Vigilantius, and Claudius, in company with the Christians of the Alpine Valleys, who later became known as the Waldenses, or Vaudois.

The Vaudois Teacher

O lady fair, these silks of mine are beautiful and rare,—
The richest web of the Indian loom, which beauty's queen
might wear;
And my pearls are pure as thy own fair neck,
with whose radiant light they vie:
I have brought them with me a weary way,—
will my gentle lady buy?

O lady fair, I have yet a gem which a purer lustre flings,
Than the diamond flash of the jeweled crown on the lofty
brow of kings;
A wonderful pearl of exceeding price,
whose virtues shall not decay,
Whose light shall be as a spell to thee
and a blessing on thy way!

John Greenleaf Whittier

Waldensian Missionaries

The poet John Whittier immortalized the scenario of a Waldensian missionary, or colporteur, in the guise of a merchant, or peddler, dressed in coarse woolen tunics and sandaled feet, selling his wares to the upper class, and then withdrawing a concealed document of the Holy Scriptures, without price. Following the example of the merchant Peter Waldo, ties always existed between the Waldenses and a milieu of merchants.

Always on the move, Waldensian missionaries could go at one period from Cologne, France, to Florence, Italy, and stay every night at the homes of brethren. Their stay was always brief, moving in secrecy, to avoid the Inquisitors, and arriving incognito in their missionary visits. Yet, their visits were received with rejoicing, called "apostles" in Germany, and in Poland received as "men who tell the truth."[21] They left behind truths that were often repeated by their recipients: "The blood of Jesus Christ His Son cleanses us from all sin" (1 John 1:7). That meant to them, no more long pilgrimages to make; no more painful journeys to holy shrines. Just come to Jesus as you are, and confess your sins directly to Him, and He will declare: "Thy sins be forgiven thee.... That ye may know that the Son of Man hath power on earth to forgive sins" (Matthew 9:5,6).

Waldensian Training

The Waldenses, were not only evangelical, but evangelistic. Like Waldo, they took seriously the gospel commission to go to all nations (Matthew 28:19,20), teaching, preaching and healing, like Jesus. But, that needed training. Way up in the Pra del Tor of the Cottian Alps, in the almost inaccessible solitude of a deep mountain pass in the Angrogna valley, was a school. It served as a college, citadel, and venue for the Annual Synod. Here the "barbes," meaning originally uncle, took their training. They committed to memory several gospels and epistles, learned several languages, and sometimes entered the great universities of Europe, where they became expert dialecticians in sharing their faith. Their training included the acquirement of some trade or profession, like Paul the tent-maker. They studied mathematics, and learned enough botany and rudimentary medicine and surgery, to bring the healing touch into their ministry. After their training they served as pastors, but every "barbe" was required to serve several years as a missionary. Usually these missionaries went out two by two, an older man with a younger man. The prospect for these young "barbes" setting out, was not some rich benefice, but instead, possible martyrdom.

Waldensian Penetration

"The Twelve Most Wanted" list of a fourteenth century Inquisitor, illustrates the widespread penetration of many nations by Waldensian missionaries. His list was not for criminals, but for twelve Waldensian ministers in Poland, Bohemia, Hungary, Bavaria, Switzerland, and Austria. Waldensian missionaries also penetrated Spain, England, and even Bulgaria and Turkey. Their healing touch extended to Austria, where Waldenses maintained a leprosarium in Neuhofen.[22] (Please see Map Illustration 3).

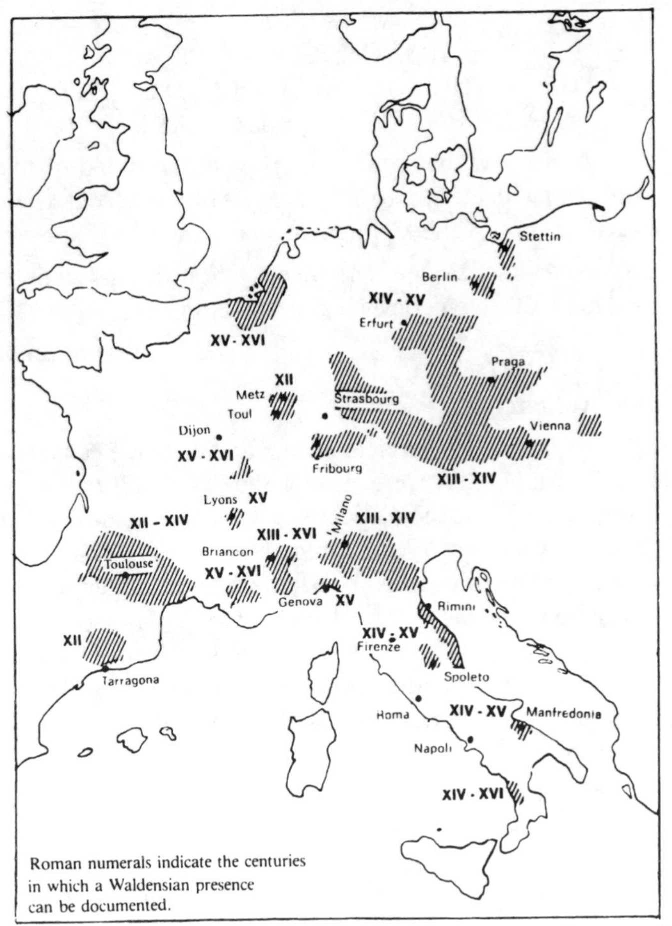

Illustration—G. Tourn, p.61

Illustration 3

The Waldensian movement in the Middle Ages

This distribution covers only the period from the 12th Century to the 16th Century, and not beyond.

Revelation Chapter Seventeen;

v. 3. So he carried me away in the Spirit into the wilderness. And I saw a woman sitting on a scarlet beast which was full of names of blasphemy, having seven heads and ten horns.

v. 4. The woman was arrayed in purple and scarlet, and adorned with gold and precious stones and pearls, having in her hand a golden cup full of abominations and the filthiness of her fornication.

v. 5. And on her forehead a name was written:

MYSTERY
BABYLON THE GREAT
THE MOTHER OF HARLOTS AND OF THE
ABOMINATIONS OF THE EARTH

> v. 6. And I saw the woman drunk with the blood of the saints and with the blood of the martyrs of Jesus. And when I saw her, I marvelled with great amazement.
>
> v.15. And he said to me, The waters which you saw, where the harlot sits, are peoples nations and tongues.

The New King James Version

"Treatise On Antichrist"

The Waldenses, not only had a clear understanding of the gospel of salvation through Jesus Christ, but they were clear on the full identification of the Great Apostasy. Having hinted on the Antichrist *yet to come* in the "Noble Lesson," the concept of the Antichrist *having already come*, is amplified and clarified, in their outstanding late thirteenth or early fourteenth century document, that escaped destruction, known as the "Treatise On Antichrist." I have a copy before me of the entire treatise translated into English, from which I will extract quotations pertinent to the identification of the harlot woman, clothed in purple and scarlet named BABYLON, that is described above from Revelation, chapter seventeen.[23]

As already noted in chapter two of this book, the symbol of a woman in Bible prophecy represents a church. The sun-clothed woman of Revelation, chapter twelve, represents the True Church, in contrast with the scarlet-clothed woman of Revelation, chapter seventeen, that represents an Apostate Church.

The Passau Inquisitor, writing about the year, 1260, bears out the Austrian Waldensian identification of the two churches:

> First, they say that the Roman Church is not the Church of Jesus Christ, but is a church of malignants.... And they say that they are the *Church of Christ*, because they *observe the teaching of Christ*, of the gospel, and of the apostles in word and example.... Sixth, that the *Roman Church is the harlot* of the Apocalypse because of her superfluous adornment.[24]

(Italics supplied)

The "superfluous adornment" of the Roman church was clearly visible in (1) the sacerdotal vestments of "purple and scarlet," and (2) the church adornment with "gold and precious stones and pearls" (Revelation 17:4).

Verse 3 of Revelation seventeen, says the scarlet-clothed woman was seated on a scarlet colored beast. Just as a rider has control over the animal he rides, so the Treatise on Antichrist, referring to the Roman church says: "He does not govern nor maintain his unity by the Holy Spirit, but by *secular power*, and makes use thereof to effect spiritual matters."

Verse 6 of Revelation seventeen, says the scarlet-clothed woman was drunken with the blood of the saints. The Treatise points out that the Roman church: "hates, and persecutes, and searches after, despoils and destroys the members of Christ."

Verse 15 of Revelation seventeen, says the scarlet-clothed woman is seated upon seas of peoples, nations, and tongues. The Treatise recognizes the universal jurisdiction of the Roman church "over every tribe, language, and nation, and all that dwell on the earth shall worship him."

Verse 4 of Revelation eighteen, says: "And I heard another voice from heaven saying, 'Come out of her my people, lest you share in her sins, and lest you receive of her plagues." The Treatise acknowledges: "the elect of God, that desire and do that which is good, are detained there as in Babylon." But they are called to: "Flee out of Babylon.... Also the Lord commands our separating...and joining ourselves with the holy city of Jerusalem...and by the Lord's help we *join* ourselves to the *Truth of Christ*," which of course is fostered by the Waldenses, who "observe the teaching of Christ" as the sun-clothed woman of Revelation 12.

Two Churches of Prophecy in Italy

In the light of this study of prophecy from Revelation seventeen and twelve, the two churches of history are the two churches of prophecy. Therefore, on the prophetic level:

(1) The Roman church is Babylon. The Waldensian church is Jerusalem, who have separated and fled from Babylon.

(2) The Roman church is the profligate woman. The Waldensian church is the pure woman.

(3) The Roman church is the scarlet-clothed woman adorned in purple and scarlet and gilded with riches. The Waldensian church is the sun-clothed woman, unadorned.

(4) The Roman church is drunken with the blood of saints. The Waldensian church are the persecuted saints driven into a wilderness experience.

(5) The Roman church is the Apostate church. The Waldensian church is the True church.

(6) The Roman church rides upon the political beast, being supported by secular power. The Waldensian church is supported by the Scriptures and spiritual power.

Such are the conclusions drawn from Revelation seventeen in contrast with Revelation twelve and in connection with the "Treatise on Antichrist."

From the "Noble Lesson" we derive that the great Apostasy is dated from Pope Sylvester of the fourth century, Constantinian era, because of its spurious offers of pardon. These are the exact words of the Noble Lesson:

> All the Popes that have been from Sylvester down to the present one, and all the Cardinals, and all the Bishops, and all the Abbots, even all such put together, have not so much power as to be able to pardon a single mortal sin. It is God alone who pardons; and no other can do it.[25]

The Treatise on 2 Thessalonians, Chapter 2

From the "Treatise on Antichrist" comes a clear identification of the Antichrist according to Paul's prophecy found in 2 Thessalonians, chapter two. The term Antichrist may mean one who is opposed to Christ, like a pagan or atheistic power. Or, it may mean one who assumes and usurps the place of Christ, instead of Christ. It is in the latter sense that Paul addresses the subject. And the Treatise demonstrates that the Waldenses, just like Archbishop Eberhard II of Salzburg, studied the history of the rise of the papacy, and found that it had shown its true colors by the thirteenth century. In fact, the Treatise gives a contemporary commentary on the Roman papacy in such a way, that Monastier says it pinpoints the pontificate of Pope Gregory VII; complete with his pretentious claims of "Dictatus," including his power to depose kings and emperors—remember the Humiliation of Canossa, 1077.[26]

Now, paying close attention to the "Treatise on Antichrist," as it relates to 2 Thessalonians, chapter two, we consider the following verses and their application to the great Apostasy, the Roman papacy. Verse 7 says: "the mystery of lawlessness is already at work." The Treatise states: "Antichrist was conceived already in the Apostle's time, yet being but in his infancy as it were."

Verse 2, of 2 Thessalonians two, says "the falling away" of the church or Apostasy comes first. The Treatise describes the papal system: "therefore though fallen away into that sin and error."

Verse 9, of 2 Thessalonians two, describes how the falling away takes place "with all power signs and lying wonders." The Treatise confirms that the Roman church makes use of "an outward confession of faith by many miracles here and there."

Here comes the climactic description of the characteristics and true colors of the Roman papacy, that fixed the attention of Monastier on Pope Gregory VII, set forth in the Treatise as follows:

> So according to the Apostle we may truly say, This is that man of sin complete, that lifts up himself against all that is called God, or worshiped and that sits himself in opposition against all truth sitting down in the temple of God, that is

> in his church, and showing forth himself as if He were God, being come with all manner of deceivableness for those that perish. And since he is truly come, he must no longer be looked for; for he is grown old already by God's permission; nay, he begins even to decay, and his power and authority is abated: for the Lord does already kill this wicked one by the Spirit of His mouth.

The Treatise continues and *summarizes* the characteristics of the Roman papacy, showing how it defrauds the Father, Son and Holy Spirit of that which is due the Holy Trinity.

First, the Roman papacy *defrauds God* of the worship due to Him, by rendering worship to creatures, whether departed saints, images, relics and the papal institution itself with its sacraments, and more especially the sacrament of the Eucharist which it adores.

Second, the Roman papacy "*robs and bereaves Christ* of His Merits—of grace, justification, regeneration, remission of sins, sanctification, confirmation, and spiritual nourishment." These are attributed to Antichrist's authority and words, to saints' intercessions, to the merits of men's own performances, and to the fire of purgatory. All of this "separates the people from Christ."

Third, the Roman papacy *defrauds the Holy Spirit* when it "attributes the regeneration of the Holy Spirit unto the dead outward work" of the two sacraments.[27] Such are the sentiments extracted from the Treatise.

To *defraud, rob and bereave* the Father, Son, and Holy Spirit of that which is due the Holy Trinity, "separates the people from Christ and leads them away"—it is a DEPARTURE FROM CHRIST. And this summary of the Treatise brings me to the climax of my thesis, citing the different DEPARTURES FROM CHRIST in the course of this book. For all such DEPARTURES FROM CHRIST result in making up the ANTICHRIST.

Finally, the "Treatise On Antichrist" pulled everything together from the prophecies of Daniel seven, 2 Thessalonians two, and Revelation seventeen, by concluding that the Roman papal system "comprised together, is that which is called Antichrist, or Babylon, or the fourth Beast, or the Whore, or the Man of Sin, the Son of perdition." Eventually the sentiments of the "Treatise On Antichrist" were to be extended far and wide, even to publication of it by the Bohemian Brethren in the sixteenth century.

Apart from the Waldenses making a great contribution to the interpretation of apocalyptic prophecy, they in fact constituted a prophetic church. They played their part in the Drama of the Ages, depicted in Revelation, chapter twelve. Their entry into prophecy is at Revelation twelve:

> v. 6. Then the woman fled into the wilderness, where she has a place prepared by God, that they should feed her there one thousand two hundred and sixty days.

> v.16. But the earth helped the woman, and the earth opened its mouth and swallowed up the flood which the dragon had spewed out of his mouth.
>
> *The New King James Version*

Prophetic Waldensian Emblem and Motto

It seemed as though the Waldenses were tied into the book of Revelation—the Apocalypse. They chose as an emblem one of the Apocalypse's seven lamp stands, representing the seven churches down through time, and surrounded it with seven stars (see Revelation 1:20). The periphery of their *lucerna sacra*-sacred torch emblem, carried the words of their motto: "Light shines in Darkness." They were going to need all that light of truth to illumine their way as they entered the Dark Ages, or shall we say the "wilderness." But, in the literal wilderness they entered "a place prepared by God." (See Photo 9 & 9a).

Prophetic Waldensian Fortress: Cottian Alps

It is no accident of nature, but Providential design, that the mountain engirdled territory of the Cottian Alps afforded a fortress of protection for the Waldenses—"his place of defense shall be the munitions of rocks" (Isaiah 33:16). No other place in Europe was so adapted to protection, as this mountain home of the Waldenses—"a place prepared by God." The wonder of it, can only be appreciated when actually seen and explored by the naked eye. I wish I could take you there for a bird's-eye view of it. This Providential mountain citadel defies any written description.

Besides the inexplicable configuration of the Waldensian mountain home, mother earth itself protected its inhabitants (Revelation 12:16). Chestnuts, an almost perfect food were plentiful, and the bark of the chestnut tree made good breastplates. The narrow defiles, slippery tracks and sudden impenetrable mists that arose, prevented the approach of the persecutors. We recall the thick dense fog that descended on Cattaneo's Crusade (1487–9) to eventually bring about the Crusade's own destruction. All told, of the 18,000 regular troops, and about as many desperadoes of Cattaneo's expedition, "few ever returned to their homes. The invaders suffered heavier losses than they inflicted."[28]

Waldenses Suffer Great Persecution

If it weren't for the protection of their mountain citadel, the Waldenses would have been crushed, just like the Albigenses, who were almost exterminated in less than fifty years. Nevertheless, papal persecution was incessant, driving the Waldenses into a "wilderness" experience, according to the prophecy. Historians have counted about thirty persecutions enacted in the Alpine valleys of the Waldenses. But, the prophecy does say "the earth helped the woman" (Revelation 12:16).

Photo 9
Waldensian Monument, Angrogna Valley, Cottian Alps, Italy
The Monument commemorates the meeting at Chamforans, 1532, when Waldenses declared their solidarity with the Reformation.

Photo 9a
The Latin motto around the emblem, or seal reads in English:
*"**Light shines in Darkness**".*

The Waldenses were mistaken, when they penned the words in the "Treatise On Antichrist" that the Roman papacy at the time of their observation "begins even to decay, and his power and authority is abated." The light of truth had not dawned upon them, that the saints shall be given into Rome's hands for 1,260 years (Daniel 7:25). Therefore, there was no way that papal authority was *abated.* And so after the Reformation was fully entrenched, the persecutors swooped down on the Waldenses, selecting a holy day to carry out their dastardly act—the "Bloody Easter" massacre of 1655. This drew a protest, and aroused British intervention.

Prophesied Help for Persecuted Waldenses

The great of the "earth helped the woman" (Revelation 12:16). Oliver Cromwell, lord protector of England, directed a relief program to the tune of over 38,000 pounds sterling. His secretary, John Milton wrote letters of state appealing to the rulers of Europe for help, and they responded. Cromwell despatched Sir Samuel Morland, who personally persuaded the Duke of Savoy to cease military operations, and so atrocities were curtailed. The massacre was immortalized by the blind poet John Milton in one of the most powerful sonnets ever written:

On the Late Massacher in Piemont

Avenge O Lord thy slaughtered Saints, whose bones
Lie scatter'd on the Alpine mountains cold,
Ev'n them who kept thy truth so pure of old,
When all our Fathers worship't stocks & stones,

Forget not: in thy book record their groanes
Who were thy Sheep, and in their ancient Fold
Slayn by the bloody Piemontese that roll'd
Mother with Infant down the Rocks. The moans

The Vales redoubled to the Hills, and they
To Heav'n. Their martyr'd blood and ashes so
O're all the Italian fields where still doth sway

The triple tyrant: that from these may grow
A hunder'd-fold, who having learned thy way,
Early may fly the Babylonian wo

The Bloody Easter massacre was seen by all *Europe* as a page out of the Apocalypse (Revelation 17:6). The saints were indiscriminately slaughtered by what Milton called "Babylon," the "triple tyrant"—the Roman pontiff with his triple crown. And that did not end the persecution, there was more to follow. Upon the Revocation of the Edict of Nantes (1685), Louis XIV, Illustrious Sun King of France, ordered the Duke of Savoy to crush the Waldenses.

Again, "the earth opened its mouth and swallowed up the flood" of persecution (Revelation 12:16). This time the literal earth of Switzerland arranged to receive Waldensian refugees. Other Waldensian refugees fled elsewhere into Europe and overseas. Strangely enough, over 200 Vaudois or Waldenses were ready to go to Cape Town, South Africa. But they declined and settled in Germany, and instead, a contingent of French Huguenots (also under the same great wave of persecution) boarded ship to South Africa.[29]

And this association of Waldenses and French Huguenots combines to form the composition of the "church in the wilderness." Another combination will be forged as we consider the Protestant Reformation in the next chapter, who also helped the "church in the wilderness" and became part of it.

(5)

THE PROTESTANT REFORMATION

MORNING STARS OF THE REFORMATION

John Wycliffe

Apparently the Waldenses were not able to effect any reform of the Roman papacy, so God directed the trumpet of reform to sound from the *universities*, that came into existence in the thirteenth century. By the year 1300, there were about fourteen universities scattered throughout Italy, Spain, France and England. God chose the Morning Star of the Reformation to arise from Oxford University England, which at that time had attained academic leadership. Since the department of theology was the most sought after among the universities, there arose a leading theologian, after many years of painstaking preparation: Dr. John Wycliffe (ca 1324–1384). The Hussites called him Dr. Evangelicus.

After receiving his doctorate, Wycliffe had an ax to grind with the Roman church on two issues: separation of the church from temporal affairs, and reform of the doctrine of salvation. The latter hit hard at the traditions of the church, which he expressed succinctly: "Of all heresies none can be greater than the belief that a man may be absolved from sin if he give money; or because a priest lays his hand on the head, and says, 'I absolve you,' for you must be sorrowful in your heart, else God does not absolve you."[1] He contended that Confession must be made to God the true Priest and not man.

Things were beginning to reach boiling point with the Roman church. In 1377 Pope Gregory XI fired back at Wycliffe with five so-called "bulls" condemning his teachings. Whereupon, Wycliffe appeared at Lambeth, faced the Archbishop, and presented his protest—*protestatio*:

> In these my conclusions I have followed the Holy Scriptures and the holy doctors, and if my conclusions can be proved to be opposed to the faith, willingly I will retract them.

Wycliffe was able to defend all his propositions with the Word of God. He asserted every man's right to read the Bible himself, and that is why his great contribution was in giving the common people the Bible (ca.1382), to read in their own native tongue—English. But, he also emphasized it should be read for the literal sense where applicable. In fact it was over the Eucharist (Mass), that Wycliffe argued that some expressions in the Bible must be understood in a figurative sense, that the bread and wine represented the body and blood of Jesus, and that the emblems were not transformed by transubstantiation into the actual body and blood of Jesus. Dilating on the dogma of transubstantiation (promulgated in 1215), Wycliffe showed that it was blasphemy, for a priest to act like the Creator. To create the bread into the actual body of Christ at his beck and call: "by what reason may you say that you make your Maker?"

The turning point in Wycliffe's life came in 1378 when the Great Schism occurred—*two popes* contended for the chair of Saint Peter, and hurled anathemas at each other. This turned Wycliffe off—he was shocked, horrified. As he studied the prophetic significance, he withdrew his allegiance. He saw clearly that the characteristics of the "little horn" described in Daniel chapter seven, verse 25, made a perfect match with the Papacy. Backed by Paul's prophecy in 2 Thessalonians, chapter two, Wycliffe declared: "the pope is antichrist here on earth!"[2]

In the same year of the Great Schism Wycliffe organized a band of itinerant preachers, that came to be known as the Lollards. Following the example of Waldo's Poor Men of Lyons, the Lollards, both lay and ordained, donned rough garb and hit the streets. With staff in hand they distributed pages of Wycliffe's Bible and tracts, and were well received by the common people. But, in 1383 Oxford expelled all Lollards from its walls, nevertheless, half of England was favorable.

Wycliffe himself was banished from his beloved Oxford, but still labored incessantly with pen in hand. He was not officially condemned by the Roman papacy during his life, but he did get his last word to the pope, a few months before his death. His letter urged, that Christians and the pope, together with his clergy, should imitate the Lord Jesus Christ in their moral lives—*imitatio Christi.*

Some important conclusions arise from the work of Wycliffe. He not only set the course of reformation to arise from the *universities*, but his attack of indulgences set the pace for a rediscovery of salvation by faith in Jesus Christ. Wycliffe's emphasis on the authority of the Scriptures, with clear-cut exegesis, was to become the battle cry of the Reformation, the Scriptures alone—*sola scriptura.*

Wycliffe's Followers: The Lollards

The followers of Wycliffe, the Lollards, molded the positions they held by prophetic interpretation. Picking up on the *day for a year principle* (enunciated by Joachim) applied to the 1,260 days of Revelation twelve, verse six, Lollard scholar, Walter Brute went so far as to say that Great Britain constituted the "church in the wilderness" for 1,260 years. Based on Daniel's prophecy, Lollards generally taught that the Roman papacy would continue for 1,260 years. Lollardism continued some time after Wycliffe, until it merged into the Reformation. But, its greatest contribution is that it set the pace for the discovery of the Antichrist, second important principle after the rediscovery of salvation in Christ. Both principles were to set in motion the great Protestant Reformation.

The Englishman that contributed to the discovery of the Antichrist was John Purvey, who led the Lollards after Wycliffe's death. Purvey's commentary on the Apocalypse (1390), based on Wycliffe's sermons, was reprinted by Martin Luther at Wittenberg in 1528, to become the first Protestant commentary on the Revelation. Luther took such an interest in it, that he wrote the Preface to this publication with these words:

> This preface, noble reader, you may understand was written by us for this reason—that we might make known *to the world that we are not the first who interpret the Papacy as the kingdom of Antichrist.* For many years prior to us, so many and so great men (whose number is large, and their memory eternal) have attempted this so *clearly and openly*, and that with great spirit and force, that who were driven by the fury of the papal tyranny into the farthest boundaries of the earth, and suffering the most atrocious tortures, nevertheless bravely and faithfully persisted in the confession of the *truth*.... Yet he [Purvey] rightly and truly pronounces the Pope Antichrist (as he is),...a witness, indeed, foreordained by God to confirm our doctrine.[3]

(Italics supplied)

John Huss

By means of an interchange of students between the universities of Prague and Oxford, Wycliffe's writings entered Bohemia. The university of Prague's policy was to make use of the books of well-known scholars of Oxford. In this way John Huss (1369–1415), rector of the university of Prague, came to imbibe the theological writings of Wycliffe, to such an extent, that they were incorporated into his own writings. And when he translated Wycliffe's greatest work into Czech for the common people to read, he got into trouble with the university authorities. The university condemned a number of Wycliffe's propositions in 1403.

Nevertheless, Huss persisted in defending Wycliffe's teachings and headed the Reformation in Bohemia. Things went from bad to worse as Rome placed Prague under interdict, and finally summoned Huss to appear at the Council of Constance in 1415. He was condemned, degraded, and escorted to the stake by the secular arm—a thousand strong.

The outcome of Huss' work was that he advanced reforms similar to Wycliffe. Buttressed by Scripture, Huss applied the symbols of the great Apostasy and mystery of iniquity, including the scarlet-clothed woman Babylon, to the Roman papacy. He even referred to mystic Babylon in a farewell letter on the eve of martyrdom.

Huss anticipated the Protestant platform—he set the supremacy of the Scriptures over the supremacy of the Papacy. At his trial he declared that he would retract any of his teachings, if they could be shown contrary to the Scriptures.

Before we leave Huss, a quick glimpse of the Council of Constance, where Huss was condemned, reveals that the Council was to heal the Great Schism, which by this time had grown to three popes. And to show their abhorrence of Wycliffe, his bones were ordered to be exhumed and burned. Over forty years after Wycliffe's death, the order was effected, and his ashes were cast into a brook. The chronicler Thomas Fuller later observed:

> Thus this brook hath conveyed his ashes into Avon,
> Avon into Severn, Severn into the narrow seas,
> they into the main ocean.
> And thus the ashes of Wyclif are the emblem of his doctrine,
> which now is dispersed all the world over.

The life, teachings, and saintly testimony of the martyrdom of Huss, who sang praises to God until the flames snuffed out his life, made a great impact upon Bohemia. Over four hundred Bohemian and Moravian nobles sent a signed protest to the Council of Constance. As the Hussite movement gained momentum, so did the opposition, in the form of Crusades against them. In some of the conflicts the hand of Providence clearly foiled the onslaught of the Crusades. Eventually, from the admixture of Hussites, Taborites and Waldenses in Bohemia, emerged a church (circa 1467) commonly called the Bohemian Brethren—*Unitas Fratrum.* At the beginning of the sixteenth century the United Brethren boasted two hundred churches in Bohemia and Moravia.[4]

SETTING FOR THE LUTHERAN REFORMATION

Papal Fifth Lateran Council

"Now no one cries out, not one objects," were the triumphant words that rang out in the oration given before the assembly of the Fifth Lateran Council, held at Rome (1512–1517).[5] Such words epitomized the sense of triumph over the pre-reformation champions Wycliffe and Huss. The only small visible thorn in the papacy's flesh, was the Waldenses in their Alpine valleys.

Extravagant words and accolades were addressed to the successful "warrior pope" Julius II as follows:

> For thou art our shepherd, thou our physician, thou our ruler, thou our husbandman, thou, finally *another God on earth*.[6]
>
> *(Italics supplied).*

In the sixth session of the Fifth Lateran Council, the next Pope Leo X, who would contend with Luther, was acclaimed: "O most blessed Leo, we hope that thou wilt come as a savior."[7]

During the closing sessions, the Council made two prohibitive pronouncements: one, prohibiting the printing of books without previous papal censorship on pain of excommunication; two, forbidding the preaching of *sermons on the coming of Antichrist*, or the judgment of the last day.

The Roman church emerged from the Council feeling that it was the New Jerusalem, just descended from heaven to be governed by the Vicar of Christ, in fulfillment of Augustine's dream, "On the City of God." Little did the Roman church realize, that before long, Martin Luther would be denouncing the church, not as the New Jerusalem, but as the scarlet-clothed woman Babylon.

Flushed with power and prestige, the Roman church strode forth from the Fifth Lateran Council in 1517, to adorn Saint Peter's with splendor and magnificence. An indulgence on a grand scale was proclaimed to finance the completion of Saint Peter's. That was the last straw to break the camel's back of the papacy. For within a few months, on the eve of All Saints day, October 31, 1517, Martin Luther posted his ninety five theses against the sale of indulgences, that launched the Protestant Reformation.

DEFINITION OF THE REFORMATION

Having described the setting for the Reformation, we need to define the Reformation, before describing the course it took. What precipitated the Reformation? Was it ignited by anticlericalism or anti-sacerdotalism, as espoused by many church historians? NO! A few historians demonstrate that the Reformation was forged on the anvil of a *twofold discovery*: one, the rediscovery of Christ and His salvation; two, the discovery and identification of Antichrist and his damnation.[8]

Bearing in mind *these discoveries* the church historian M. Merle D'Aubigne wrote: "The different phases of the Reformation succeeded each other in the soul of Luther, its instrumental originator before their accomplishment in the world."[9] Luther discovered Christ and His salvation before 1517. He discovered Antichrist and his damnation before 1520. On these two epochal discoveries rested the entire Reformation.

COMMENCEMENT OF THE REFORMATION: DISCOVERY OF CHRIST

"I am no vain dreamer," said John Huss, "but hold for certain that the *image of Christ* shall never be effaced. They wish to destroy it: but it shall be painted afresh in the hearts of gospel-preachers better than myself. And I, awaking as it were from the dead, and rising from the grave, shall rejoice with exceeding great joy."

How could the image of Christ be painted in the heart of Martin Luther? He knew not how. But, after studying law for four years, to the surprise of all, he plunged headlong into the solitude of an Augustinian monastery, subscribing to the vows of poverty, chastity and obedience. It was the long established notion among the more serious, that the convent was the place, and its prayers, penance and self-mortification the means, whereby one may obtain salvation and the favor of God. There are many today, who likewise think that salvation comes by joining a church, and following all the rules and regulations.

As Luther's conviction of sin deepened, so did his own works deepen to obtain pardon and peace by means of fasting, long prayer vigils, and scourgings approaching self-mortification. It was in a resultant state of collapse, that von Staupitz, the pious vicar-general of the monastery found him, and *opened the Scriptures* to Luther's mind. Anyone in search of the truth of salvation, must inevitably be driven to "search the Scriptures, for in them you think you have eternal life; and these are they which testify of Me" (New King James, John 5:39). Can you noble reader relate to that?

These were the words of Staupitz that made a deep impression on Luther's mind, and brought peace to his troubled soul, rather than the rigors of his monastic life. "Instead of torturing yourself on account of your sins, throw yourself into the Redeemer's arms. Trust in Him, in the righteousness of His life, in the atonement of His death.... Listen to the Son of God. He became man to give you assurance of divine favor. Love Him who first loved you" (1 John 4:19).[10] Thus, the Scriptures were opened to Luther's mind.

Luther began to trust in the righteousness of Christ, imputed to him. He now beheld the glory of Jesus, not as an avenging judge, but "full of grace and truth" (John 1:14) "forgiving iniquity and transgression and sin" (Exodus 34:6,7). Recognizing that he was a *great sinner, desperately in need of salvation*, is fundamental to Christianity. But, one must accept forgiveness after confession is made, and that is what led Luther to exclaim: "O happy sin which has found such a Redeemer."[11]

Luther was still a true son of the Roman church and had no desire to be anything else, when he was sent on a mission to "Holy Rome," ostensibly to strengthen his faith. As Luther mingled with monks and citizens, he beheld opulence and luxury mixed with profanity, dissipation, and debauchery, that belied the title "holy." Nevertheless, he went through all the ceremonial motions required of the faithful in Rome. He was horrified to hear that if there were a hell, Rome was built upon it.

When Luther left Rome, he had virtually turned away also in heart, it was so foreign to his developing Christian experience. Upon his return from Rome, Luther received from the University of Wittenberg the Doctor of Divinity degree (1512). At the same time he received, as it were, his vocation as reformer, because he vowed on the conferral of the degree to defend the Word of God. It was the authority of Scripture alone, that would undermine the foundation of the Roman church and launch the Reformation.

Luther, after receiving his doctorate, gave himself as never before to the study of the Scriptures. He preached, and he taught. The tenor of his message was to learn a new song; "Thou Jesus, art my righteousness; I am thy sin: Thou hast taken on thyself what was mine: Thou hast given me what is thine."[12]

The deep study of the Scriptures that Luther loved, led him to lecture on the Psalms, Romans and Galatians. "The just shall live by his faith" (Romans 1:17), was a passage of Scripture that Luther pondered over for a long time, to grasp its full meaning. When he grasped the meaning he said: "I felt myself to be reborn and to have gone through open doors into paradise." One thing he did learn from this text, was that holy pilgrimages to Rome, acts of penance, veneration of relics and images, intercession of saints, purchases of pardon, were mere crutches to support a tottering faith. All of these could be dispensed with. All one needed to be justified by God, was faith in the merits of Christ, and not the works of man—all one needed is faith alone, *sola fide*.

Luther had been DRAWN TO CHRIST, thereby he made his *discovery of Christ and His salvation*. The reformation that had taken place for Luther himself, was to be *passed on to Western Europe*. And the opportunity that presented itself was the grand sale of indulgences for Saint Peter's in Wittenberg, Germany, by John Tetzel. The purchase of an indulgence from the pope provided full remission of all sins, even contemplated sins; no confession necessary; valid for loved ones in purgatory.

Luther's response to Tetzel was immediate and swift. He posted on the door of the Castle church, Wittenberg, 95 theses, or propositions against the sale of indulgences, designed and intended for debate the next day at the university. Since Luther adored the pope, his theses were not intentionally written to attack the pope. Nevertheless, all Europe was electrified. Within a few weeks the theses were copied, translated, printed, and circulated throughout Christendom. The impact produced a mighty shock that rippled across Europe declaring in effect: the pope's utter insufficiency to confer forgiveness of sin or salvation. Second, the theses set forth Christ's all-sufficiency in salvation. A mortal shock too, was inflicted, although Luther did not know it yet, against Papal supremacy.

As a result of Luther's discovery of Christ and His salvation, followed by his preaching and presentation of the 95 theses, Europe awoke from a long slumber. And to put it in the words of Melanchthon: "as if a new day had risen on Christian doctrine, after a long and dark night."[13] It was not just a new day that had dawned, but a new discovery of Christ and His salvation, as if in response to the Greek call, "Sir, we would see Jesus" (John 12:21).

CONTINUATION OF THE REFORMATION: DISCOVERY OF ANTICHRIST

Following Luther's *discovery of Christ and His salvation* came the *second phase* of the Reformation, his *discovery and identification of Antichrist* and his damnation.

Luther considered himself still a faithful son of the Roman church after the posting of his 95 theses. In fact he was dumbfounded, when he heard that the pope was still in favor of the efficacy of indulgences—he had thought that the pope was on his side.

Luther Before the Leipzig Disputation

Luther pondered over the association of the pope with the abuses of indulgences. And in the next year following, 1519, after receiving a brief from Dr. John Eck regarding an upcoming public debate, Luther resorted to an *examination of the origin, foundation, and character of papal Rome*. Luther wrote to an important figure, "I have been turning over the decretals of the popes, with a view to the ensuing debate at Leipsic; and would whisper it into thine ears that *I begin to entertain doubt*, (so is Christ dishonored and crucified in them) whether the Pope be not the very Antichrist of Scripture."[14] (Italics supplied).

Luther apparently did not study at this time the interpretation of prophecy applied to papal Rome, written by others *before* his day. Reminiscences of his visit to Rome, observations of the then present papal system, its origin, development and characteristics, compared with the prophecies of Scripture, led him to profound conclusions. Luther did not, as it were, regurgitate, or bring up what others had said *before* him. And after all, isn't that the way, you noble reader would like to examine the question. In fact, that is what has been portrayed for the reader of this book. In the beginning of the book you were taken on a guided tour of Saint Peter's in Rome. Next, you were given a history of the rise of the church at Rome. Then the prophecies of Daniel, Paul, and John the Revelator, were compared and applied, to arrive at convincing conclusions.

Luther and the Leipzig Disputation, 1519

The Leipzig Disputation between Eck and Luther came to a head. Apart from the proximity of Leipzig with Bohemia, where Huss perished, Eck drove

Luther into a corner by associating his teachings with Wycliffe and Huss—thereby securing Luther's condemnation as a heretic. Luther asserted that it was not necessary for salvation, to believe that the Roman church was superior to all others, whether this came from Wycliffe or Huss. Furthermore, appealing to Scripture which contained the vital principle of the Reformation, Luther averred that even a simple layman armed with Scripture, is to be believed above pope, or council without it. Luther declared that he was ready to defend the truth with his blood, and that he wanted to believe freely, without being a slave to the authority of any one, whether council, university, or pope.

After the Leipzig Disputation Eck returned to Rome to secure the excommunication of Luther by the pope. In the meantime the encounter at Leipzig had strengthened Luther's *growing conviction* of the identity of the Antichrist. When Luther's friends begged him to hold back one of his primary works, the tract entitled, "The Address to the German Nobility," he said that it had already been printed, and wrote the following in reply:

> We here are of the *conviction* that the *Papacy* is the seat of the *true and real Antichrist*, against whose deceit and vileness all is permitted for the salvation of souls. Personally I declare that I owe the Pope no other obedience than that to Antichrist.[15]

(Italics supplied)

Luther Burns the Papal Bull

Barely two months after writing the above letter, Luther received the papal bull of condemnation known by its opening words—Exsurge Domine. Sixty days later (December 10, 1520), Luther, in the presence of a crowd of students, doctors and citizens, burned the papal bull, along with the canon laws and decretals, declaring, "As thou hast vexed the Holy One of the Lord, may the eternal fire vex thee."[16]

Such was the heroic act of Luther, that riveted the attention of Europe on the *second phase* of the continuation of the Reformation—the *discovery of Antichrist* and his damnation. It struck a special chord in the Drama of the Ages—Christ versus Antichrist. And remember, that Luther revealed the Antichrist and wrote about it, in the face of the two prohibitions that emanated from the Fifth Lateran Council. Luther certainly disturbed the peace and tranquillity that was voiced at that Council.

Luther's Gallant Stand

Luther's gallant act attracted the attention of papal Rome, and they followed up on that episode. Luther was summoned to appear before the imperial Diet of Worms, presided over by the newly appointed Emperor Charles V of Germany and the Holy Roman Empire. Although charged with heresy, Luther was given the opportunity to recant. This was a momentous occasion that would determine the course of history. The destiny of the Reformation hung in the balance. The battle lines were drawn between Christ and Antichrist. Luther stood his ground and declared unequivocally before an august assembly:

> I cannot submit my faith either to the pope or to the councils, because it is clear as the day that they have frequently erred and contradicted each other. Unless therefore I am convinced by the testimony of Scripture or by the clearest reasoning, unless I am persuaded by means of the passages I have quoted, and unless they thus render my conscience bound by the Word of God, I cannot and I will not retract, for it is unsafe for a Christian to speak against his conscience.

Luther's German Bible

No sooner did Luther leave the Diet of Worms, than he was spirited away by a band of horsemen, prearranged by the elector, Duke Frederick of Saxony. He was conveyed to the castle of Wartburg, an isolated mountain fortress. It was from this rocky Patmos that he translated the New Testament into vernacular German, for his beloved countrymen to read by the thousands. This was Luther's greatest gift, and won for him great acclaim. Another great accomplishment was that Luther's complete Bible contributed to standardizing the German language.

While Luther worked on translating the Old Testament into German, his interest in the prophecies received a new impetus. The book of Daniel so impressed him, that he rushed it to the press before publishing the other Old Testament books, sensing the urgency of the times, and the identification of the Antichrist.

Luther's Historical Unfolding of Prophecy*

As for the other apocalyptic book, the Revelation, Luther gave an outline of his views on the meaning of prophecy, in his complete edition of the German Bible published in 1534. He believed that the book of Revelation presented *a preview of the history of the Christian Church*, with reference to the *two witnesses* of Revelation , Chapter eleven, and the *sun-clothed woman* of Revelation , Chapter twelve, who flees to the wilderness from her persecutors. Although he was not clear on the time element (as was Osiander) of the *sun-clothed woman*, he was clear that she represented the *True Church*. But he did not define who, or what comprised the true church. Luther believed Revelation, Chapter thirteen, was *a preview of the history of papal Rome*. In the outline of views in the 1545 edition of the German Bible, he identified the scarlet-clothed woman Babylon with papal Rome (Revelation 17). The eighteenth chapter of Revelation Luther believed was the destruction and damnation of papal Rome. On 2 Thessalonians, chapter two, Luther did not pin the Apostasy, or Antichrist on any single being. He believed the Antichrist is collective, an institution, the papal succession is a system, and he was clear that it would arise in the church: "The Turk cannot be Antichrist, because he is not in the church of God."[17]

How gratifying to find Luther's historical base for Apocalyptical prophecy. His historical unfolding of the prophecies of Revelation 11, 12 and 13 reminds us of the historical interpretation introduced by Joachim (Chapter 3) at the close of the twelfth century—an epochal breakthrough. Luther's identity of Revelation 13, 17 and 18 with the Roman papacy was also widespread among Reformers.

Universal Interpretation of Papal Apostasy*

Besides Luther's contribution of the German Bible, he wrote over 300 treatises. But, about four hundred writers produced 1,500 treatises, to swell the tide of literature from over forty centers during the German Reformation. This kept the people informed in the running battle between Christ and Antichrist. It represented the greatest doctrinal war ever waged over Bible truth, to that time. The general tenor of its polemic was the *discovery and identification of the Antichrist*. And hosts of Reformers wielded the "sure word of prophecy," as the sharp two-edged sword of the spirit. They inaugurated an *era of truth and liberty*, the likes of which the world had never seen before. The view that the Roman church was Babylon and the Lawless One, the Great Apostasy, or Antichrist, seated in the Christian Church, was *universally held by the Reformers of the sixteenth century*. The universality of their testimony attests to the authenticity of their interpretation of Apocalyptical prophecy *as absolute truth.*[18*] (Please See this Footnote listing).

Such truth was considered so vital, that it became an article of faith in some church creeds. I submit the statement found in the Westminster Confession of Faith (1647), ratified and established by Act of Parliament, which reads:

> There is no other head of the Church but the Lord Jesus Christ: nor can the Pope of Rome, in any sense be head thereof; but is that Antichrist, that man of sin and son of perdition, that exalteth himself in the church against Christ, and all that is called God.[19]

Involvements of the Reformation

God worked in sundry and mysterious ways to kindle the fires of the Protestant Reformation. He kindled the fires of the Reformation in the *universities* of Oxford, Prague and Wittenberg; in the *cities* of Nuremberg, Zurich and Geneva; in the hearts of the *princes* who protested at the Diet of Speier in 1529; and in the hearts of *kings and queens*—and that was not all. God also caused the Reformation to spread like wildfire from country to country: Lutheranism from Germany to Denmark and Sweden; Calvinism from Switzerland, added its distinctive characteristics to the reformatory movement in Bohemia and Moravia, Hungary, France, Netherlands, Poland, and Scotland. The Reformation in England blazed like a bonfire.

Thus, emerged the Reformation church as the composite sun-clothed woman of the Apocalypse, yet to be persecuted by the scarlet-clothed woman of the Apocalypse. But thank God that "the earth helped the woman" (Revelation 12:16) in various ways. The Reformation was helped and aided by the Renaissance and Nationalism. Above all, the Reformation was stimulated by the printing press, that pried open the minds of people to receive the great truths, found in the innumerable vernacular Bibles printed, and in the literature, that came off the press like the leaves of autumn.

Conclusion

On that triumphant note we take a breather, and pause for a little reflection, and see where we have arrived. In the Prologue of this book was an appeal to present day Protestantism, to take a long hard look back to its roots. To recall *how and why* Protestantism arose, and *recover* a precious truth that has been *lost* to Protestantism. I believe I have delivered on that appeal. Protestantism arose upon the rediscovery of Christ and His salvation, and upon the discovery and identification of the Antichrist. The latter discovery is based upon "a more sure word of prophecy." That means prophecy has progressive historical fulfillment. One looks for fulfillment along the whole long line of history. This is in harmony with the prophetic principle laid down by Jesus: "I have told you before it takes place, so that when it does take place, you may believe (R.S.V. John 14:29). With the advance of time comes the unfolding of prophecy as historical events.

Be that as it may, would you be surprised to find that modern Protestantism has *lost* or rejected (1) the identification of papal Rome as the great Historical Apostasy or Antichrist, together with (2) the historical interpretation of prophecy. Thereby, as it were, Protestantism has thrown out the baby with the bath water. And so, now, I am going to tell you how this happened. I shall give a historical outline showing how these precious truths were *rejected and lost* to Protestantism. It was by means of the Roman Catholic Counter Reformation that these truths were lost.

Something that may shock the reader, is to realize that these precious truths of the identity of the Papal Apostasy, and the principle of continuous historical interpretation of prophecy, took *three centuries* to be searched out, and brought to a climax with Luther. It then took another *three centuries* to be discarded by Protestantism. The next chapter will reveal the part played by the Counter Reformation and modern Protestantism in bringing about the loss of these precious truths.

(6)
THE COUNTER REFORMATION

The little David of the Protestant Reformation had not slain the Roman Goliath. Neither was it going to sit back and lick its wounds. It sallied forth with gargantuan strength to oppose the Reformation in what has come to be known as the Counter Reformation of papal Rome.

The Counter Reformation was by and large a fourfold Roman Catholic offensive against the Reformation. It included: (1) the formal inauguration and work of the Order of Jesuits; (2) the revival of the Inquisition and all out bloody persecution; (3) the actions and decrees of the Council of Trent; (4) the Catholic counter-systems of prophetic interpretation.

1. The Order of Jesuits

The Counter Reformation is said to have started with the papal authorization of the new Order of Jesuits under the leadership of Ignatius Loyola, in 1540. The Dominican and Franciscan Orders had somewhat fallen into disrepute. It was high time that the Roman church receive a new infusion of zeal. Loyola, of Spanish descent through a family of knights, who served in the royal court of Ferdinand and Isabella, rose to the occasion. He formed a fighting Order, a holy militia for the defense and prosecution of the faith, and top notch education. The Order, backed by unconditional obedience to the pope, was disciplined by Loyola's Spiritual Exercises, and went forth with military precision to turn the world upside down—and they nearly did that.

Jesuits, intent on capturing the world for the Papacy penetrated India, at the port of Goa, the East Indies, China, Japan, Africa and America. By the time Loyola died, the Order, a thousand strong, had established one hundred colleges.

Turning their attention on the Protestant world, Jesuits would fight Protestants with its own weapons—preaching, educating and reforming, and they believed in time all would be won. While Protestantism was losing some of its vitality because of its dissensions, the Catholic revival was gaining strength. Jesuit education was soon established in Vienna, Koln, Ingolstadt and Lyons. Jesuits took advantage of the weak spots of Protestantism, such as the peasantry throughout France, Poland, and even Hungary. They gained the favor of princes, to endow the new colleges, and they themselves became entrenched in the universities. The munificence of the King of Spain, Phillip II, was evident in the foundation of twenty two Jesuit colleges. By 1615, the Jesuits had over 13,000 members, and were operating in thirty two provinces. There is no doubt that they blunted Protestant advance to some degree, and regained a large share of lost territory.

2. Increased Persecution

The Counter Reformation was almost a Spanish movement throughout. From Spain emanated both the Jesuits and the Spanish Inquisition under *royal control*, which meant untold thousands perished in Spain and the Low Countries. The Roman Inquisition was revived as the *tribunal for the whole church* in 1542. The Counter Reformation reached a high water mark, with the Massacre of Saint Bartholomew (1572) against the French Huguenots, and the Bloody Easter Massacre of Waldenses (1655). It overflowed as a flood of persecution against the Huguenots and Waldenses with the Revocation of the Edict of Nantes (1685). And that only tells part of the story, of the redoubled effort of papal Rome to crush Protestantism in the Counter Reformation. But, it also revealed clearly the scarlet-clothed woman Babylon, 'drunken with the blood of the saints" (Revelation 17:6).

3. Papal Council of Trent, 1545 to 1563

The third force of the Counter Reformation was the Council of Trent, that convened at Trent in the Austrian Tyrol. This was the longest held Council in the history of the Roman church—commencing 1545 and concluding 1563. The Council was ostensibly called to reform abuses, but to the chagrin of the Emperor Charles V, no serious reform had been effected at the end of the first assembly. In fact no reform of abuses or reform of doctrine was forthcoming. The effect of the Council, was that the Roman church simply dug in its heels, tied up all loose ends of its teachings, received the pope's benediction and approval, and crystallized its actions into decrees that became the *permanent and unchanging law* of the Roman Catholic Church. And woe betide anyone who opposes the Council's decisions! In the closing session the Cardinal exclaimed, "Anathema to all heretics," to which the delegates answered, "Anathema, Anathema."

Here are some of the most significant decisions against the Protestant faith, which made the breach with Protestants absolutely final.

At the fourth session of the Council of Trent, April 8, 1546, it was decided that Holy Scripture and Tradition were equal in authority. Tradition was placed on a par, with the same pious affection (Latin: *pari pietatis affectu*) and reverence with the Holy Scriptures. Though, by implication Scripture is made subservient to Tradition, through insistence that it *be understood only by tradition*—meaning a continual inspiration, that resided particularly in the unanimous teaching of the Church Fathers. Notice what Jesus said about tradition: "Why do you also transgress the commandment of God because of your tradition? And in vain they worship Me, teaching as doctrines the commandments of men" (New King James, Matthew 15:3,9).

Further decisions were taken relative to the Holy Scriptures. The traditional Canon of Scripture, including the Apocrypha, was accepted, the Vulgate being the authoritative text. No one, but the church, could expound Scripture. Cardinal Pole carried the decision with these words: "Our beliefs and our worship, in their entirety, depend upon Tradition."[1]

Cardinal Pole pointed out at the Council, that Justification by Faith was at the root of most of Luther's errors on the seven sacraments, the power of the keys, and even on indulgences and purgatory. On the question, is Justification inherent or imputed, Lainez, who was the elected second general of the Jesuit Order, called for the vote, and imputed righteousness was defeated 32 to 5. The Protestant assertion of an absolute assurance of salvation was also rejected.[2]

While the Italians were in the majority at the Council of Trent, the Council owed its impetus to the Spanish. Without us considering any other decisions from the Council of Trent, it was an epochal event for the Roman church, and every Roman priest today is sworn to receive, profess, and maintain its decisions. Only two cardinal tenets have since been added—the Immaculate Conception of Mary in 1854, and the Infallibility of the pope, and the universality of his episcopate in 1870. Another Marian doctrine of the Assumption was added in 1950, when it was promulgated by the pope *ex cathedra*.

4. Roman Church's Counter-systems of Prophetic Interpretation

The fourth force of the Counter Reformation was the Roman Church's counter-systems of prophetic interpretation. It is to be noted that the *first phase* of the Protestant Reformation, namely the *discovery of Christ and His salvation*, was rejected by the Council of Trent. More specifically the Council rejected Luther's teaching of Justification by Faith alone, without the added ramifications of the works of men created by the Roman church. However, the *second phase* of the Reformation, namely the *discovery and identification of the Antichrist*, was not at all discussed at the Council of Trent. It fell to the lot of two astute Jesuit scholars, Alcazar and Ribera, after the Council of Trent, to deliberately bend and twist the Holy Scriptures in order to destroy the Protestant identity of the Antichrist as papal Rome. To confuse the Protestants, if not the world, they invented *two counter-systems* of prophetic interpretation. Bent on eradicating the identity of the Antichrist by devious means was no issue, because Jesuits believed that the end, justified the means.

The Spanish, who had dominated the scene of the Counter Reformation, were out to play their last hand effectively, to play havoc with the interpretation of prophecy—and in this they succeeded to future generations. The Spanish scholars Alcazar and Ribera DEFLECTED the incriminating finger of prophecy pointed by Daniel, Paul and John at the Roman papacy. Alcazar *deflected* the existence of the *Antichrist to the distant past*, the early Roman period—thus introducing the *Preterist* counter-system of prophetic interpretation. He achieved this, by the publication in 1614, of a 900-page commentary on the Apocalypse.

On the other hand Ribera *deflected* the existence of the *Antichrist to the distant future*, into a minuscule space of time prior to the consummation and Second Coming—thus introducing the *Futurist* counter-system of prophetic interpretation. He achieved this, by the publication in about 1590, of a 500-page commentary on the Apocalypse.

Hence, the battle lines were drawn, the mighty phalanx of two counter-systems of prophetic interpretation, to do battle with the Protestant continuous *Historicist* system of prophetic interpretation. The outcome of this conflict was to have dire consequences.[3]

A protracted discourse on the consequences of Preterism is beyond the scope of this book. But, the consequences of Futurism have direct bearing. So, let's consider first of all the gist of Ribera's prophetic interpretation. Ribera denied the Protestant Scriptural Antichrist (2 Thessalonians 2:4) as seated in the church of God—asserted by Augustine, Jerome, Luther and many reformers. He set on an *infidel Antichrist, outside the church of God.* Ribera laid aside the collective Antichrist institution taught by Protestants, for a *single individual* who would rebuild the temple in Jerusalem, abolish the Christian religion, deny Christ, be received by the *literal Jews* , pretend to be God and conquer the world—all of which has *no foundation in Scripture.* And on top of it, all would be accomplished in 1,260 literal days, a literal 3½ year period (1260 divided by 360 = 3½). He paralleled the sun-clothed woman in the wilderness with the persecution of the Antichrist during that 3½ year period (Cf Daniel 7:25; Revelation 13:5; 12:6,14). It is highly improbable that such stupendous accomplishments were possible in a minuscule period of time—the likes of which have never been seen in history. Such are the wild fancies of one who deviates from Scripture (Please See Illustration 4).

Besides the novel interpretation of the Antichrist, Ribera struck at the foundation of the historical interpretation of prophecy. Ribera's principles of interpretation went haywire. What was obviously *symbolic* language in Revelation, he made *literal*, such as with the 144,000, and the 1,260 days. The four digit figure 1,260 suggests a long period of time on the *day for a year scale*, as first delineated by Joachim, and continued through the Reformation. But Ribera changed the obvious symbolic language to read literally 1,260 days.

Alcazar relegated the Antichrist to the distant past, by making it stop altogether *short* of the rise of Papal Rome. Ribera, on the other hand, hurled his Antichrist in one giant leap over the immense interval of time, taken up by the long history of papal Rome, to an indefinite position in the distant future, just *before* the consummation.

Such a giant leap left an immense interval of time in between, in which prophecy had nothing to say, and had naught to do. Ribera assigned the first

L. E. Froom, II, 508

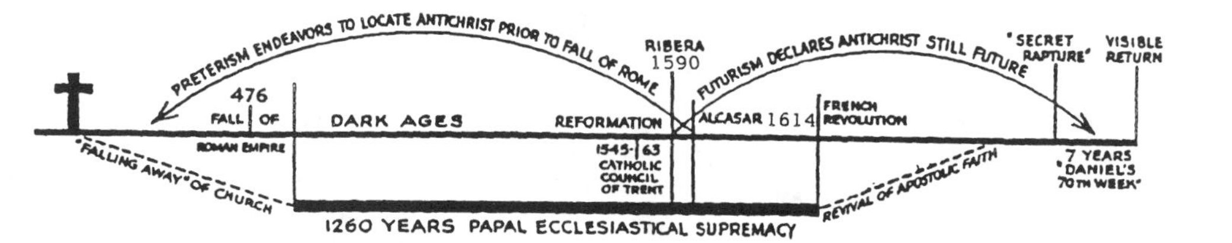

Illustration 4

Deflection of Antichrist either Backward or Forward

Alcazar deflected the existence of the Antichrist to the distant past—the early centuries of the Roman era. Ribera deflected the existence of the Antichrist to the distant future—a miniscule 3½ year period. These manipulations are on either side of the Middle Ages and the Reformation period, or on either side of the 1,260 year period of Papal Dominance.

few chapters of Revelation to ancient Rome, and then without any Scriptural warrant or sign, hurled chapters eleven to fourteen way into a future diminutive period of three and one half literal years. Thus, he introduced a *vast* gap, a silent immense interval of time, a vast silent gulf, that proponents of Futurism are loathe to mention, lest it call their bluff. It is this GAP theory that permeates Futurism's interpretation of all apocalyptic prophecy.[4]

It was the intention of Pope Gregory XIII to drive home the two counter-systems of prophetic interpretation. He appointed the famous Italian Cardinal, Jesuit Robert Bellarmine, to teach controversial theology to aspiring missionaries. His book, "Controversies" championed Alcazar and Ribera, and became the arsenal for all future exposition, or defense of the faith and order of the Roman church. The growing proclamation of these counter-systems later drew the attention of the Protestant Dr. Drue Cressener.

Cressener Opposes Counter-systems and Fixes Period of Papal Dominance

Cressener not only opposed these counter-systems pointedly, but took the opportunity to *strengthen* the Protestant position, by his work dedicated to Queen Mary in 1690, titled, "A Demonstration of the First Principles of the Protestant Applications of the Apocalypse." While fine-tuning the parallel prophecies of Daniel 7 and Revelation 13 in this book, Cressener was the first to make the landmark discovery of the duration of papal Rome. He dated it from the Justinian era, when Justinian pronounced the Roman pope the Universal Head of all churches, and inserted it in the Civil Code. Thus, Cressener placed the *dominance of papal Rome* from Justinian's era, about 538, adding 1,260 years, and reaching to "a little before the year 1800."[5]

Jesuit Ribera's Futurism Adopted by Modern Protestantism

The Futurism of Ribera never posed a positive threat to Protestants for three centuries. It was virtually confined to the Roman church. But, early in the nineteenth century it sprang forth with vehemence and latched on to Protestants of the Established Church of England. From 1826 Dr. Samuel R. Maitland the former lawyer, and later librarian to the Archbishop of Canterbury, proceeded in pamphlet after pamphlet to demolish the foundations of Protestantism, as built on the historical prophetic testimony of the Word of God.

Maitland was followed by the Irish scholar J.H. Todd who acknowledged drawing his arguments from Maitland. In like manner, John H. Newman, the famous High Church Anglican convert to Roman Catholicism, who received a Doctor of Divinity degree from the pope, including a cardinal's hat, acknowledged drawing his arguments from Todd. And Newman was one of the prime movers of the Oxford Tractarian Movement, born in London, the prime objective of which was to "unprostentize the Church of England."

Such attacks on Protestantism left an almost indelible impression upon the minds of people, and "left Protestantism consequently all open to the charge of unjustifiable schism; and the Papacy all open to the Catholic desires, and aspirations of the Tractaters for reunion."[6] Thus, "a Romeward movement was already arising, destined to sweep away the old Protestant landmarks, as with a flood."[7]

Owing to the trend as outlined above modern day Protestantism has lost sight of precious truths, namely, (1) the identification of papal Rome as the great Historical Apostasy, or Antichrist, and (2) the historical interpretation of prophecy—Historicism.

Having outlined how the Futurism of Ribera entered the ranks of Protestantism from a general point of view, I shall now outline the entrance more specifically. Like Ribera, Maitland opted for an *individual infidel Antichrist* who was yet to arise *outside the church of God*; "and sit for 1,260 literal days in a literal temple of brick or stone, proclaiming himself to be God."[8] For more than ten years Maitland's polemical productions had the ring of a lawyer, discrediting and debunking the Reformers and the Protestant Reformation. He felt it was a grave mistake to accuse the Roman church of apostasy from the faith of the New Testament, and expressed no deep sympathy with the great work of the Reformation.[9]

Todd and Newman repeated the arguments of Maitland like a refrain. Todd's ponderously documented work, is in reality a series of negations of the whole Protestant Church. His negations range from the time of the Waldenses and their unquestionable, "Treatise On Antichrist," to the Lollards, Hussites, Lutherans, Calvinists, Huguenots, Puritans, including many other Protestant interpreters of prophecy, and the Confessions of Faith, etc. All of these he declares were in: "gross error as to the meaning of prophecy, and the character of the church of Rome."[10]

How could these men and their followers, claim to be Protestants, and yet disavow the Protestant Reformation, and refer to it as an "unwarrantable schism?" These detractors and repudiators have simply each one, shot himself in the foot. He, who is a true Protestant cannot reject the "more sure word of prophecy," identifying the papal Antichrist. A true Protestant *cannot deny* "that which all the Reformers held to be the testimony of the Spirit against that idolatrous church."[11]

In 1898 Joseph Tanner related the tragedy of modern Protestantism in these words:

> It is a matter for deep regret that those who hold and advocate the *Futurist system* at the present day, Protestants as they are for the most part, are thus really playing into the hands of Rome, and helping *to screen the Papacy from detection as the Antichrist.* It has been well said that 'Futurism tends to obliterate the brand put by the Holy Spirit upon Popery.' More especially is this to be deplored at a time when the *Papal Antichrist seems to be making an expiring effort to regain his former hold on men's minds.*[12]

(Italics supplied)

Before closing this enlightening chapter in search of truth, may I point out, that while the diatribes of the heavyweights Maitland, Todd, Newman and others were extolling the virtues of Futurism, giants of Historicism rallied to engage in the titanic struggle for truth. One such giant was Edward B. Elliott, graduate of Trinity College, Cambridge, a scholarly prophetic expositor of the century. His four volume monumental work, 'Horae Apocalypticae' (Hours with the Apocalypse), was occasioned by the Futurist attack on Historicism. Without an equal in exhaustive research in its field, this work ran through five editions from 1844 to 1862. Elliott's work stands as a Monument, to the truth of the Protestant continuous Historicist system of prophetic interpretation.

Recovery and Restoration of Vital Truths

Be that as it may, we cannot just stand in awe before a Literary Monument. But, we can *recover* truths lost to Protestantism caused by the onslaught of the Counter Reformation. Recognizing the unscriptural, devious, deliberate invention of the Preterist and Futurist counter-systems of prophetic interpretation, it is not difficult to recover and accept the historical system of prophetic interpretation. This Historicist system, held from Joachim's time, through the Protestant Reformation, and beyond to the present time has *no devious origin*.

Modern Futurists separate chapters four through nineteen of the Revelation, and place them to be fulfilled in a diminutive period of time at the consummation, becoming absolutely irrelevant to the Christian believer. Historicists, on the other hand, can rejoice that those chapters have *relevancy*, because we are living through them now. As a true Protestant we are in good company with our Protestant Fathers, standing on a firm foundation of continuous historical unfolding of prophecy. Hence historical fulfillment is the true interpreter of prophecy.

Having *recovered* and recaptured the precious truths of the identification of the papal Apostasy, resting on the firm foundation of Historicism, we move on to reclaim other truths bypassed by Protestantism. You, noble reader, will rejoice and be glad to discover these truths in the next chapter, as we are DRAWN TO CHRIST in a fuller, deeper experience.

(7)
THE RADICAL REFORMATION

Origin of the Anabaptist Movement

The Radical Reformation had its rise in Switzerland. At the opening of the sixteenth century Switzerland was a free country. It was a Confederation of thirteen cantons owing allegiance, neither to the German emperor, nor to individual lords. However, the city council was the seat of authority.

The term radical has been applied, because it was not entirely orthodox by the standards of the times. On the other hand, there were extremes like the Munsterite Uprising. Nevertheless, a movement should not be judged by the excesses of some. By and large the movement did not have a revolutionary spirit, but rather a missionary spirit. Some Reformers rejected the movement as radical, because they did not agree with the views of the Reformers. Owing to the disagreement they were called Anabaptists—meaning rebaptizers.

The Anabaptists, however, did not consider themselves as rebaptizers. They rejected infant baptism that they might have experienced, believing that adult believers' baptism was not a second baptism, but the only genuine baptism.

The question may arise, then, how did radicals bring about a Reformation? Putting aside the paradox, we will now see that the Anabaptist movement arose as an *extension* of the Reformation—born in a barn! Well not quite so. Born in a large meeting hall of over nine hundred friends of reform, proposed by the Zurich Council, and designated as the Second Zurich Discussion, 1523. The meeting was called to discuss the use of images, and the sacrifice of the mass. Such a meeting was the prelude to the city of Zurich siding with the Reformation in a few years time. It was also the prelude of the organization of the Anabaptist movement.

Three salient lights of Anabaptism, who were friends, or associates of the Reformer Huldreich Zwingli, were present at the Zurich Discussion. The truths that were to shape the extension of reform, were beginning to germinate at this meeting. Dr. Balthasar Hubmaier, theologian and pastor at Waldshut, who had received his doctorate in the same year as Luther, who learned his theology at the feet of Dr. John Eck, was present at the meeting. He had conferred earlier with Zwingli, presenting a reform package with reference to infant baptism, but at the meeting he challenged the efficacy of images and the mass. Conrad Grebel, Zwingli's former protege, desired that the priests should be instructed in reference to the mass. Zwingli replied that the Zurich Council would decide what course they should pursue. Simon Stumf, like a lightning rod, ignited the atmosphere of the meeting: "You have no authority to leave the decision with the Council."

In spite of the Council mandate, Hubmaier removed images and holy objects from his Waldshut church, and celebrated the Lord's Supper in German, in all simplicity, without ritual, and as a commemorative service. He also published a tract relative to the Lord's Supper entitled, "The Sum of a Perfect Christian Life." Thus, the simplicity of the Lord's Supper became an Anabaptist article of faith.

Origin of Free Church Concept

Stumf did not come away from the Zurich Discussion as lightly as Hubmaier did, he was dismissed from his pastorate, and banished by the Zurich Council. His statement at the Zurich Discussion was not appreciated, because it was the spark to ignite the *separation of the church from the state*. And it was this issue, that was to separate the Anabaptists from the Reformed church. Since the time of Constantine, church and state had been united. Lutheranism and Calvinism had been successful in removing the pope from its social scheme, but it could not imagine a society without a strong leader. So the pope was replaced, and power and authority was vested in a local prince, or city council. Luther, Calvin, and Zwingli, relied on the government to put their reforms in place. In essence Stumf and his associates were advocating a great truth, they were the originators of the concept of the FREE CHURCH, separate from state control.

Restoration of Apostolic Church Concept

Stumf was indeed a thorn in the flesh of the Zurich Council's side, because even before the Zurich Discussion, he had first discussed the concept of the church with Zwingli. The current belief was that the entire European society was a great Christian society—the *corpus Christianum*. This concept of the church was accomplished, because the church routinely baptized all infants. Therefore the body of the church encompassed all members of society, believers and unbelievers, whether casually, or by conviction, or by coercion—it mattered not. Such a conglomerate church presented problems. The church could not demand the high ethics of Christ's Sermon on the Mount, from those who were only Christians because they were citizens, or because they were baptized at infancy. The outcome for the church was that morality was at a low ebb. And since Zwingli was intent on continuing such a church, Stumf and his associates were outraged, and looked for reform to institute a *new pure church of committed believers only*, modeled directly from the *apostolic age of the New Testament*. The paradigm of the church was to be found in the Acts of the Apostles, from chapter two onwards.

The Anabaptists aimed at a restoration of primitive godliness, the pristine purity of the early gospel. Anabaptists sought for that, which in the gospel "stirs the consciences of men to be ill content, with anything short of full conformity with the ethical standards, set forth in the teachings of Jesus."[1]

The Anabaptists viewed the church as a free and voluntary association of *genuine believers*—free to enter, free to leave, and free from state control. Genuine Anabaptists were also among the first to consistently uphold the truth of RELIGIOUS LIBERTY.

Church of Committed Believers, Upon Confession of Faith and Baptism

Membership within the body of the Anabaptist concept of the church was open to genuine, committed believers—those who are obedient to the call of God; who are truly repentant; who have separated from the pleasure-loving, wealthy, proud and violent world (1 John 2:15–17); who have taken up their crosses to follow Christ (Matthew 10:38); who have, upon personal confession of faith, been baptized into Christ, as a sign of His death, burial and resurrection, and are prepared to walk in newness of life (Romans 6:3–6). This embodies a genuine personal commitment, nothing casual, and is the very *essence of salvation.*

After that digression, explaining the great truths contributed to Christianity by the Anabaptists, we continue the Anabaptist saga, and how they arrived at these truths, especially the truth of BAPTISM, key to the entire movement—if not all Christianity.

Grebel, a young man in his twenties, Felix Manz, and other young men came together frequently, to study the Scriptures for mutual edification. At one of these gatherings, they came to the conclusion that infant baptism was not Scriptural, and that baptism was for believers upon profession of faith. They began to publish their discovery, and also found others of like-mind. Furthermore, they rejoiced to come across tracts on the subject, circulating in Zurich, by the noted theologian Dr. A. Carlstadt, companion Reformer of Luther. The swelling tide of opposition to infant baptism soon reached the ears of the Zurich Council, who called for a public discussion in the Council Hall, January 17, 1525. As a result of the meeting they published a mandate, ordering parents to initiate baptism of all children, who had not received the ordinance of baptism, within a week, or suffer banishment. Thus, infant baptism, an ordinance of the church, became an *ordinance of civil authority.*

The Course of the Anabaptist Movement

January 21, 1525, was a red-letter day, but not before the Zurich Council had read the riot act—forbidding Grebel and Manz to discuss the subject of baptism, and giving their four associates a week to leave the canton. That night, was the red-letter day, when Anabaptism was *officially born*, as a result of the Zurich Hall meeting a few days before. Georg Blaurock, a former priest, confessed his faith and his sins, and asked Grebel to baptize him, by pouring water over his head. Blaurock in turn baptized the other men meeting in Manz's home. Shortly after, Wilhelm Reublin went to Waldshut, just thirty miles from Zurich and there baptized Hubmaier, and sixty others. During the Easter season of that same year, 1525, Hubmaier, in turn baptized 300 converts. These events marked the beginning of the Anabaptist movement, and were almost like a page out of the Acts of the Apostles, "and the Lord added to the church daily such as should be saved" (Acts 2:47).

What a glorious scene it was, to behold even lay preachers taking the message of the gospel to those hungry for the Word, baptizing them, and setting them to witness to others. In lonely cottages, in the valleys, and along mountain slopes people were gathered together. The Bible was read, lessons of salvation in Christ moved the hearts of hearers. It was a new gospel to thousands, and souls responded with tears of repentance, and turned their lives over to the Lord. They asked the privilege of *confessing their faith in Christ*. Then, like Ulimann, whom Grebel first baptized by *immersion*, they retired to some mountain stream, to be baptized like the eunuch in the Acts of the Apostles, and went on their "way rejoicing" (Acts 8:37–39), and converts multiplied by the hundreds around Appenzell.[2]

Because of the phenomenal early success of the Anabaptists, reaction set in. Zwingli published a tract titled, "Baptism, Rebaptism, and Infant Baptism." Hubmaier got hold of a copy and replied, July 1525, "Concerning the Christian Baptism of Believers." It carried Hubmaier's motto: "Truth is immortal."

This was one of the greatest truths to arise at the time of the Reformation, the very pillar of the Christian faith, one that towers above all else, for, said Jesus: "Except a man be born of water and of the Spirit, he cannot enter into the kingdom of God." (John 3:5). It is astounding how this monumental truth was bypassed, rejected, opposed, and lost to the Reformed church and the Lutheran church and others, and is still not accepted by many Protestant churches today. Nevertheless, considering all the persecution the Anabaptists suffered, the truth of Baptism was not suppressed, it is immortal, it has transcended all attacks, and today, because of it a great body of believers have been DRAWN TO CHRIST.

Hubmaier's tract on baptism was widely circulated, and exploded like a bomb—its shrapnel penetrating many minds and bringing conviction. Something more drastic had to be done to stem the tide of Anabaptist advance. Brushing aside any thought of the right of the individual to be free, to follow the dictates of his own conscience, the Zurich Council confirmed an earlier edict with more vigor, that Anabaptists should be punished by DROWNING, issued November, 1526.

Hubmaier immediately wrote to Zwingli denouncing the edict. In fact, Hubmaier, on another occasion had written a tract against intolerance and the burning of heretics. To produce such a tract would immediately place the author on the black list. So, no-one dared take the chance. Hubmaier's tract, and daring, then stands out in bold relief, against a background of unspeakable intolerance, as a monumental appeal for religious toleration. I am persuaded then to share some of the sentiments. In a haunting series of propositions he wrote:

> Thirteen: The inquisitors are the greatest heretics of all, since, *against the doctrine and example of Christ*, they condemn heretics to the fire.
>
> Fourteen: For Christ did not come to butcher, destroy, and burn, but that those who live might live more abundantly....
>
> Twenty eight: To burn heretics is in appearance to profess Christ, but in reality to *deny Him*....
>
> Thirty six: It is clear to everyone, even the blind, that a law to burn heretics is *an invention of the devil.* 'Truth is immortal.'[3]

(Italics supplied)

Thanks Hubmaier! You have immortalized the truth of religious toleration!

To return to the Anabaptist narrative, Hubmaier's appeal availed nothing. The Zurich Council's edict to punish Anabaptists by drowning went into effect. Why drowning? Because it poured contempt on the Anabaptists, and derided their practice of baptizing by immersion in water. The slogan of the day, expressed the fate of Anabaptists with ghoulish humor: "He who dips, shall be dipped—by drowning."

Such oppressive measures sealed the fate of the Swiss Anabaptist movement. The Zurich Council was out to destroy the Anabaptist heresy, root and branch. They even commenced a correspondence with Augsburg and Constance regarding Anabaptists. Other cantons in Switzerland followed the example of the Zurich edict. Such were the forces mustered against the so-called heretics, in spite of what men like Reformer H. Bullinger said: "I see nothing in them but earnestness, and I hear nothing of them except that they will not take an oath, will not do any wrong, and aim to treat men justly. In this it seems to me, there is nothing out of the way."

The suppressive measures of drowning and the stake, Swiss Anabaptists bravely faced, but the loss of their leaders weakened their cause. The obituary roll of three of the original half dozen leaders of the Swiss Anabaptist movement reads: Felix Manz, the Hebrew scholar, in whose house the first baptism took place, was the first martyr who sang praises to God before being drowned, 1527; Conrad Grebel, natural death, 1526; Georg Blaurock, first one baptized, burned at the stake, 1529.

By the time of the death of Zwingli, 1531, the Reformation had taken root according to Zwingli's plan, in the cantons of Zurich, Berne, Basel, and

Schaffhausen, and the state church had virtually silenced the Anabaptist movement, except for some small enclaves. But, the Anabaptist movement had spread elsewhere, to Moravia and Austria, particularly through the charismatic evangelist Hans Hut. So did persecution spread to these lands, and in the matter of four days after the notable Protest of the Princes, at the Diet of Speier, the Diet enacted an imperial decree, 1529, to exterminate Anabaptists.

As a result thousands of Anabaptists were slain in Austria under papal persecution, let alone Protestant. Therefore, the Anabaptist movement was crushed in Austria, practically disappeared in South Germany, and was consolidated in the Netherlands by Menno Simons.

Anabaptist Belief: A Contribution to Christianity

The Anabaptists made a contribution to Christianity on the subject of Christian living—the fruitage of Christian experience. They brought this charge against the Reformers:

> By the Evangelicals there is not real earnestness manifested;...the Word of God *bears no fruit*: and all this because they preach justification by faith only, but do not *urge good works*; they always represent Christ as the One who has done enough for us, instead of setting him forth as *our example to follow*.[4]

(Italics supplied)

To accept Christ as Savior is only the beginning of faith. Obedience to Christ as Lord, is an integral part. Included in obedience is to *follow Christ's example*. Jesus said; "Take My yoke upon you and learn from Me, for I am gentle and lowly in heart, and you will find rest for your souls" (New King James Matthew 11:29). Anabaptist writings are replete with following the example of Christ, well expressed as follows:

> Let Christ Jesus with His Spirit and Word be your teacher and example, your way and your mirror.

Luther himself had taught that works are not the means of salvation. Faith is the *root of salvation*. Works naturally follow as the *fruit of salvation*. Luther said; "Faith is a living, restless thing. It cannot be inoperative. We are not saved by works; but if there be no works, there must be something amiss with faith." Obedience and the following of Christ's example is not legalistic, but rather the fruitage of faith. Said Luther; "He who does not obey has no belief or faith."

Anabaptists took seriously John 13:34: "A new commandment I give to you that you love one another." In concrete terms it meant, love your enemies, do good to them that hate you, do not fight (they were pacifists), do not retaliate (modeling after the Sermon on the Mount). It meant community of property in aiding the needy, comforting the sorrowful, and preaching the gospel.

Furthermore, in obedience to Christ they endeavored to give ear to the ten commandments, the fruitage of moral Christian living, ably expressed by Menno Simons:

> We teach from the mouth of the Lord that if we would enter into life, we must keep the commandments; that the love of God is that we keep His commandments...even though we have always confessed that we cannot be saved by means of anything, other than by the merits, intercession, death, and blood of Christ.

Bearing in mind the contribution of Christianity, by the Anabaptists' balanced view, of the relationship of faith and works, and following the example of Christ in obedience to Him, it is no wonder that another episode developed in the story of the Anabaptists in Moravia.

But before we get into that episode, we need to note by July, 1526, Hubmaier and his wife settled in Nikolsburg, Moravia, belonging to the princess of Liechtenstein. Here the tolerant, protector of the Anabaptists, Prince Leonhard von Liechtenstein, was baptized by Hubmaier. An estimated 12,000 Anabaptists gathered in Nikolsburg under Hubmaier's influence. But, Hubmaier's work came to an untimely end, when he was tried in Vienna and burned at the stake, 1528. His wife was drowned in the Danube three days later. Hubmaier's writings were under twenty four titles, a sizable Anabaptist contribution. And in memory of his name, he was leagued with the great: Luther, Calvin, Zwingli, and Schwenkfeld—on the black list of the Council of Trent, of course.

If Protestants can be numbered among those who constitute the sun-clothed woman in the wilderness (Revelation 12), certainly the Anabaptists belong to that invisible church with the significant qualification: "they did not love their lives to the death" (Revelation 12:11) recalling their heroic martyrdoms. Besides, they also found refuge in the "wilderness" of Moravia, with its vast forests, affording protection for the persecuted. Furthermore, the great men of the earth, nobles, and the princess of Liechtenstein for a time "helped the woman," Revelation's metaphor for the true church (Revelation 12:17).

Sabbatarian Anabaptists

Luther was not enamored with Sabbatarian Anabaptists, whom he identified as living in Austria and Moravia. And yet, were they not living up to his own definition of the true church: "Where God's Word is purely taught there is the true church?"

Apparently Sabbatarian Anabaptists were among the thousands of Anabaptists that gathered around the chief center, Nikolsburg, Moravia, in 1529. Anabaptist protector, Prince Leonhard von Liechtenstein, whom Hubmaier baptized, "held to," or favored the Sabbatarian Anabaptists.[5]

In fact Liechtenstein had asked the Sabbatarians to submit to him a statement of their belief, which they did quite readily. After receiving the statement, Liechtenstein passed it on to C. Schwenkfeld for his comments on it. Schwenkfeld's comments turned out to be a refutation in book form (1532), yet it preserved Sabbatarian argumentation. Another refutation by V. Crautwald cropped up about this time, preserving Sabbatarian belief. It is from these extant refutations before me, that I will quote and glean the reasoning of the Sabbatarian Anabaptists.[6]

Since Anabaptists were fully committed to the teachings of Jesus, in obedience to Him, emphasis on obedience to the ten commandments would naturally follow, as already noted by Menno Simon's statement above. Simons said, "we must keep the commandments," with reference to Matthew 19, verse 17, and John 15, verse 10. Anabaptists reasoned that the ten commandments are found in Exodus, chapter twenty, written on tables of stone by God at Mount Sinai, yet these principles were kept by Abraham (Genesis 26:5) long before, and are intended for all generations, for all time, to "remain until the end of the world" (Matthew 5:17–19).

It follows naturally, that if one gives close attention to the ten commandments, one will soon come across the fourth commandment that reads: "Remember the Sabbath day, to keep it Holy." This is what the Sabbatarian Anabaptists discovered, and that, with the observance of the ten commandments, went also the observance of the Sabbath on Saturday. Thus, Schwenkfeld conceded: "The strongest argument of the Sabbatarians is the number of the ten precepts,...which neither Christ nor the apostles have tried to change.... From which they conclude: if the Sabbath is void, all the other commandments are also."

Sabbatarians contended from James, "If someone says he keeps the whole law, but fails in one point, he has become guilty of breaking all of it; he has become a transgressor of the law. Pray tell, can or may the Sabbath be an exception?" The breaking of any commandment, including the Sabbath, constituted sin, and it is sin that separates from God and Heaven—the continuation of which constitutes eternal loss. Therefore, Sabbatarian Anabaptists, instead of breaking the law and sinning, declared: "Through faith we establish the law, Romans Three; therefore also the Sabbath" (Romans 3:31).

Sabbatarian Anabaptists supported the origin of the Sabbath from the beginning (Genesis 2:1–3), to continue through the forty years wilderness wandering (Exodus 16), "to be kept as long as the world stands" (Exodus 31:13,16,17). They explained how to observe the sabbath, which they claimed to have restored (Isaiah 58; Nehemiah 13), presenting it as essential to Christian reform.

Sabbatarian Anabaptists pointed out, that the Scriptures contained overwhelming evidence in favor of the Sabbath. On the other hand, they stressed the paucity of textual evidence for Sunday. Appealing to *history*, they asserted "all assemblies of Christians were held on the Sabbath for many years after Christ's time," including "all early fathers" of the church. They continued: "Pope Victor and Emperor Constantine are the first ones who ordered that Sunday should be kept, it is also issued in the Decretal; but God instituted and ordered the Sabbath." Sunday is therefore manmade and is devoid of sanctity.

Since Anabaptists followed the example of Jesus in baptism, it would not be long for them to follow the example of Jesus in observing the Sabbath (Luke 4:16).

Likewise, if Anabaptists, bent on re-establishing the *apostolic church*, incorporated an odd belief like community of property into their faith, what's to say they would not incorporate the Sabbath, that "Paul and the apostles" observed (Acts 13:14,15,42–44; 15:21; 16:13; 17:1,2; 18:1–4). The fact that the apostles observed the Sabbath, gave strength to their concept of the apostolic church and the Sabbath truth.

The Sabbatarian Anabaptists were steeped in Scripture, and may well have fulfilled Luther's statement: "Where God's Word is purely taught there is the true church."

English Baptists

Owing to the suppression of Anabaptists in continental Europe, it took over three-quarters of a century for the truth of baptism to arise in England. John Smyth, who had studied for the Anglican priesthood separated, gathered a group of English nonconformists, and to escape the Anglican authorities, emigrated to Amsterdam, Holland. Here they befriended the Dutch Waterlander Mennonites of Anabaptist descent. Either from the influence of the Mennonites or his own study of the Scriptures, Smyth learned the truth of baptism. Whereupon, in 1609, Smyth confessed his own faith, baptized himself by pouring, and then went on to baptize Thomas Helwys, and several others present. This small group became the first English Baptist Church on Dutch soil, modeled after the primitive Apostolic church. But the congregation was short-lived, it split, one part joined the Mennonites with Smyth, who died in 1612. The other part of the congregation returned to England in 1612, led by Helwys, to become the first Baptist church on English soil. Helwys gave strong, but short leadership, he expired four years later.

English Baptists generally believed that the church is composed of true believers, separated from the world, baptized into the fellowship of the church, upon profession of faith. From the start, Smyth and Helwys advocated freedom of conscience. Helwys' book constituted the first comprehensive case for religious toleration in the English language. Baptists built upon such initial powerful advocacy, to lead other dissenters in the cause of religious liberty, until the Toleration Act of 1689. Smyth's book also advocated an innovation, which the General Baptists continued to practice until the eighteenth century.

It was the *ordinance of foot-washing* (John 13:13–17), following the lead of Anabaptists, first practiced in Hubmaier's Waldshut church, 1525.

Smyth believed that baptism was not exclusively a requirement for church membership, as it was a "sign" of the true church. Smyth's first congregation believed, along with other Separatists, that the Church of England and the Roman Church was not the true church, but the Great Apostasy.

Furthermore, *baptism by immersion*, which became the mode in the 1640's, suggested *ultimate obedience to Christ*, with strong Biblical backing. And that is what characterized Baptists as Biblicists. Early Baptists argued solely from Scripture, whereas Anglicans, Presbyterians, Congregationalists, and Roman Catholics argued from Scripture, tradition and sometimes from reason. Hence, the debate over believer's baptism raged on, well into the eighteenth century. The Protestant principle of *sola scriptura*—the Scripture alone, still contends for the truth. Eventually, consolidation of the English Particular Baptists took place in the London Confession of Faith, 1644, published by seven churches, mainly from the area around London. This meant identification with main-stream English Protestantism, separate from continental Anabaptism. Yet Anabaptist tenets of faith were duplicated in the main.

American Baptists

A number of Puritans had left England, since the landing of the Pilgrims in 1620, to settle in the Massachusetts Bay Colony of North America. There they hoped to establish a "Zion in the wilderness." By 1631, when Roger Williams and his wife arrived near Boston, the colony had an Anglo-Saxon population of about five thousand, among whom were settlers described as being tainted with the virus of Anabaptism.

Roger Williams arrived in Boston with Baptist leanings, promptly forfeited the offer to be minister of the large Boston congregation, and settled for an independent church in Salem. At Salem he began to preach separation of church and state, and religious liberty. This got him into hot water with the General Court of the "Zion in the wilderness," and in 1635 the General Court ordered him to leave Massachusetts. He left Massachusetts, before being arrested by soldiers.

In the thick of winter, Williams fled into the wilderness forests for fourteen weeks, finding shelter in hollow trees, or in the wigwams of Indians, whose friendship he had cultivated before, and whose language he had learned. Such friendship resulted in a gift of land by the Narragansett chief, which he promptly named Providence, and expressed his gratitude: "For God's merciful Providence unto me in my distress."

In 1638 the First Baptist Church of Providence was organized. Ezekiel Holliman, a member of Williams' Salem church, baptized Williams, and he then baptized Holliman and ten others. The cardinal tenets of faith upon which the church was organized included: complete separation of church and state; complete freedom of conscience, stating that persecution for the cause of conscience was contrary to the doctrine of Jesus Christ; men are accountable to God alone for their religious creed.

After all was said and done, Williams remained with the Baptist church for about four months and then withdrew completely, to care for the affairs of the colony, and create the first pure democracy. By 1644 Rhode Island had grown to four communities, Providence, Warwick, Portsmouth, and Newport. The latter city's congregation of Baptists was the catalyst for Baptist expansion into Connecticut, Massachusetts and the middle colonies. By the time of the Baptist Association in 1707 the combined membership of twenty Baptist churches, amounted to five hundred.

The year 1644 is significant in the history of New England for two reasons. First, because Williams secured a Charter from England, that gave the Providence Plantations full power to rule itself, and granted that "all men may walk as their consciences persuade them,...without molestation, in the name of Jehovah their God, for ever and ever."

The second reason why the year 1644 is significant, is that the Massachusetts Bay Colony, from which Williams was banished, continued its oppressive way: It passed a law associating offenders with the heresy of European Anabaptists. The law sentenced to banishment, anyone opposing the baptism of infants.

In the meantime Roger Williams offered his colony as a haven for the persecuted, particularly the Baptists from Massachusetts, and the Quakers. Furthermore, he offered political freedom and strict separation of church and state. There was to be no class consciousness, Catholics, Jews, and even nonbelievers were given full citizenship. In 1654 Williams was elected President of Rhode Island, which he held for three terms.

It is to the credit, however, of John Clarke, of the Newport Baptist Church, that a Charter was issued from England for the *larger* Rhode Island colony in 1663. This charter was the first legal sanction to full religious liberty in America, fostered by Dr. John Clarke.

Finally, the Massachusetts Bay Colony was granted a new Charter by Charles II of England in 1682, similar to the Rhode Island Charter, that proclaimed full religious freedom and toleration. The later history of Massachusetts indicates the influence of Baptists, as champions of religious liberty.

In 1779 a delegate to the constitutional convention, requested Baptist leader, Isaac Backus, to write his views as a draft bill of rights, for possible inclusion in the new Massachusetts constitution. Although the draft of Backus on religious liberty was not accepted in 1779, it was incorporated into the state constitution of Massachusetts in 1833.

A contemporary of Backus, by the name of John Leland, is believed to have talked about religious liberty and separation of church and state, and may have influenced Thomas Jefferson and James Madison. Such Baptist sentiments may well have influenced the framers of the First Amendment of the Bill of Rights, majestically articulated: "Congress shall make no law respecting an establishment of religion, or prohibiting the free exercise thereof."

English Seventh Day Baptists

The term Protestant Reformation reflected, among others, reform or change, to bring to the notice of the churches the need to accept the *newly discovered truths*, arising from a concerted study of the Holy Scriptures. Since the Scriptures were more readily available, a concerted study ensued, resulting in an *age of Biblicism*. Furthermore, the development of the Free Church concept, set people's minds free from the restraints of the established churches, to pattern their lives after the Scriptures—the only *rule of faith and practice*. Strangely enough, along with the discovery of believer's baptism, came the discovery of the Biblical Sabbath of the fourth commandment. And in line with the Biblicism of the age, the Sabbath was buttressed with a list of Bible texts, following the Scripture proof text method. These two discoveries combined to form the Seventh Day Baptist Church.

Although there were sporadic outbursts in writing, on the Sabbath question, from individuals within the Church of England, it was not until the English Baptists were established, that the Sabbath truth found its way among Baptists. It is likely that individual members of established Baptist and Independent congregations, at first broke away to keep the Sabbath in private group worship. The eventual location of many Seventh Day Baptist churches was also in the vicinity of Baptist churches.

The emergence of Seventh Day Baptists was during the great decade 1650–1660, when at least ten bona fide Seventh Day Baptist churches were known to exist from London to Northumberland. By the turn of the century Seventh Day Baptists listed eighteen churches in England.

Like other Baptists, the Seventh Day Baptists attracted well-to-do middle class adherents. The most prominent concentration of Seventh Day Baptists was in London, with three churches at Bell Lane, Pinners' Hall, and Mill Yard. The latter church was among the first to be organized, back in 1654, and is still in existence today. Prominent names, like court physician Dr. Peter Chamberlen, the martyr John James, and the pastor William Saller, had connections with the Mill Yard church. Two other churches at Colchester, and Baintree, in the neighboring county of Essex, made up the concentration in and around London.

Persecution of Seventh Day Baptists

Seventh Day Baptists of the mid-seventeenth century faced much opposition and persecution. The government of the time did not always look carefully into one's personal beliefs, and so guilt, merely by some loose association with political thought, or philosophy, was common ground for persecution. Such was the case of the several imprisonings of Anglican clergyman Francis Bampfield, (M.A. Oxford). Nevertheless, while in prison he was convicted of the Sabbath truth, and preached as often as sixteen times a week to other prisoners and visitors, forming a church, and then he died in prison. His brother Thomas, on the roster of Sabbatarians, shared a similar fate, and went to jail in Ilchester, after having been a member of Parliament, and speaker of the House of Commons in 1659.

Guilt by association, sealed the fate of the Seventh Day Baptist minister, John James. On Sabbath—Saturday, October 19, 1661, James was dragged from his pulpit, on the charge of uttering treasonable words against the king from Scripture. he was unjustly tried, and convicted to be hung, drawn, and quartered. James made an eloquent confession of faith, committed his life to God, and was executed. "His quarters were placed over the city gates, and his head was set upon a pole, opposite the meetinghouse in which he had preached the gospel."[7]

Writings of Seventh Day Baptists

From the start of the Seventh Day Baptist movement, their writings drew fire from opponents, and I mean that literally. In 1650 James Ockford published in London, "The Doctrine of the Fourth Commandment, Deformed by Popery, Reformed and Restored to its Primitive Purity." The book caused such a stir in the city of Salisbury, that the mayor asked the speaker of the English Parliament, what should be done, since it undermined the observance of the Lord's Day—Sunday. A committee of the Parliament ordered that all copies of the book be burned—apparently only one escaped the fiery ordeal.

In spite of what happened, a pithy writer E. Fisher, came to the defense of Ockford, with his book, "Christian Caveat," against the Puritans, and it ran through five editions. Thus, a titanic struggle ensued to get the Sabbath truth out, and scores of books were written by capable Seventh Day Baptist writers.

Champion of Christianity, Chamberlen M.D., Searches Out Truth

The best known name associated with Seventh Day Baptists was Peter Chamberlen M.D., of distinguished French Huguenot descent, brilliant court physician to three Stuart kings—James I, Charles I, and Charles II. As a Fellow of the Royal College of Physicians, he was a pioneer in scientific midwifery, a reformer in medicine, and in many ways he was far ahead of his age. He tried to introduce medical measures, which only materialized long after him. He is reputed to have improved, if not to have invented obstetrical forceps.

Apart from Dr. Chamberlen being a reformer in the field of medicine, his impressive epitaph declares: he was a Christian, keeping the commandments of God and the faith of Jesus (Revelation 14:12), having been baptized, and keeping the seventh day for the Sabbath above thirty two years. In the role of a Reformer he championed the Sabbath truth, serving as a pastor for a time, and writing and debating to bring the Sabbath to the forefront. He even presented the Sabbath in a prophetic setting from Daniel, Chapter seven, verse 25 quote:

> He shall speak pompous words against the Most High,
> Shall persecute the saints of the Most High,
> And shall intend to *change times and law*.
>
> *The New King James Version. (Italics supplied)*

Chamberlen acknowledged that Daniel seven, verse 25, described the characteristics of the "little horn," that arose among the ten horns of the Roman beast power. He recognized

(1) that the little horn entity was the papal Roman Apostasy that made pompous, blasphemous claims and pretensions, which were against the Most High;

(2) that papal Rome would persecute the saints of the Most High;

(3) that papal Rome would intend, or attempt to *change times and the law of the Most High*. Namely, papal Rome would tamper with the law of God, the ten commandments, more specifically the *fourth commandment*, instituting Sunday, the first day of the week, thereby obliterating the Sabbath—Saturday, the seventh day of the week. Thus, the time scale of God, and the fourth commandment was molested, altered, *changed* as a whole, by the Roman Church.

This light of truth dawned only upon those who observed the Sabbath; those who observed Sunday, would not see the significance of this clause in Daniel seven, verse 25. Chamberlen's discovery of the attempted *change* of the Sabbath by the Papacy (reference: Council of Laodicea in Chapter 3) was not his alone, it was shared by his contemporaries in the faith: the Bampfield brothers, Saller, and others who promulgated it with zest.[8]

American Seventh Day Baptists

To conclude the story of Seventh Day Baptists, it is possible that the intolerant atmosphere that prevailed in England, influenced Seventh Day Baptists, Stephen Mumford and his wife, to emigrate to Rhode Island. Here they attended Dr. John Clarke's Baptist Church in Newport, in 1664. During the next year Newport members, Samuel Hubbard and wife, embraced the Sabbath truth. By 1671, the number who accepted the Sabbath grew to five, whereupon they severed their membership with the mother Baptist church, and joined with the Mumfords, to organize the first Seventh Day Baptist Church in Newport.

Prominence came to the Newport Seventh Day Baptist Church, the first on American soil, in that it produced two governors of Rhode Island. Benedict Arnold, who followed after Roger Williams, was the first. The second who followed later, was governor Richard Ward (his son Samuel also became a governor).

But, even more prominent, is the fact, that in its early days, the Newport Seventh Day Baptist Church was a missionary church, that helped to spawn congregations in Westerly, Providence, New London, Narragansett, Plymouth Colony, and Martha's Vineyard. By 1802 the Seventh Day Baptist Church as a whole, reported about two thousand members in twenty churches, scattered from New England to Georgia.[9]

(8)
THE GREAT REVIVAL

The fires of divine truth were well-nigh extinguished upon the altars of Protestantism at the close of the seventeenth century. Christianity was steeped in formalism, passiveness, and leaning toward rationalism. What was needed, was a revival, and three men were born right at the start of the eighteenth century, destined to head a revival—Count Zinzendorf, John Wesley, and Jonathan Edwards.

Pietism

But, before these three revivalists, Champions of Christianity, played their part in the Search for Truth, Pietism prepared the way. Like the Reformation of the sixteenth century, this Pietistic revival began in Germany, through the leadership of Phillip Spener and August Franke, a professor of Divinity at Halle, in Saxony. A wonderful revival of the spirit of genuine piety in the city, and University of Halle, accompanied the movement. Pietism, simply stated, described a movement in which people would be DRAWN TO CHRIST—and I'm all for that! It meant knowing Christ in a *personal way*—as a personal Savior. More than that, it meant *falling in love* with Christ, so well expressed by Zinzendorf: "I have one passion, tis He!" Pietism on the individual, personal level, meant obedience to Christ, to *walk* with Him, separate from the pleasure-loving world—Oh, for a closer walk with Christ!

Count Zinzendorf and the Moravians

Count Zinzendorf, whose godfather was Spener, and whose tutor was Franke at Halle, imbibed Pietism. After completing his secondary studies at the University of Wittenberg, he went on a tour, and encountered his Savior—an experience that was to plot the course of his life. His attention was riveted on a beautiful art piece in a museum, entitled "Behold the Man," a portrait of the thorn-crowned Savior, with the inscription: "I have done this for you; what have you done for Me?" There and then Zinzendorf pledged, "I have loved Him for a long time, but I have never actually done anything for Him. From now on I will do whatever He leads me to do."

Having attained his majority, Zinzendorf purchased an estate, to become a refuge and settlement for the persecuted, located near Dresden in Saxony, on the border with Bohemia and Moravia. By 1727 the settlement attracted over three hundred refugees, and an interesting set of circumstances, prompted the organization of what the English call the Moravian Church—a combination of the revived United Brethren with Zinzendorfian Pietism. The settlement was named Herrnhut—the Lord's Watch, complete with a night watchman, hourly testifying through the night, the eternal Presence and watch of the Lord. Zinzendorf's favorite thought was God's "blessed Presence." The doctrine of the Presence of Christ permeated the atmosphere of Herrnhut—God was on their lips, they lived in His Presence. And as lonely Moravian missionaries, at the far flung ends of the earth, like Surinam, they were powerfully comforted by Christ's Presence.

Zinzendorf portrayed a piety that differed somewhat from that of Halle, in its special *cheerful looking to Christ.* It extended to a cheerful, *self-sacrifice*, and a piety looking to devoting one's entire life to witness and service of Christ—in answer to the portrait inscription: "What have you done for Me?" The response to this at Herrnhut was immediate and continuous, resulting in the greatest surge of missionary expansion of all time.

Phenomenal Moravian Missions

In the decade 1732 to 1742, under review, over seventy untrained Moravian missionaries from about 600 Herrnhutters rallied to the call, and invaded the lands of slaves, heathen, and primitive people, like storm troopers for Christ. Herrnhut sent batches of missionaries to reach the slaves of the West Indies, and as they died off, under deplorable conditions, missionary reinforcements were sent in—such was the *self-sacrificing devotion.* There was no let up, they penetrated Greenland, Lapland, Surinam, and the Guinea Coast of Africa. They reached South Africa, at the Cape Colony's Genadendal (Glen of Grace) mission to the primitive Hottentots, still in existence today. They entered Amsterdam's Jewish quarter, the North American Indians, Ceylon, Romania, and Constantinople. Upon the death of Zinzendorf in 1760, 226 Moravian missionaries had been sent out.

Zinzendorf charged the Moravian missionaries to preach nothing else, but Jesus Christ and Him Crucified (1 Corinthians 2:2), His Holy Life, and His abiding Presence, as the substance of their gospel message, and this resulted in 3000 baptized converts. After Zinzendorf's death the missionary work went on, for example establishing Schoenbrunn (Beautiful Spring) in 1772, the first Ohio settlement. The Moravian missionary movement made such an impact on the world, that it inspired the Baptist and Methodist mission outreach, and led to the formation of the London Missionary Society, and the British and Foreign Bible Society.

Moravian Christian Life-Style

Life in Herrnhut was happy, but very busy—five full days of work and study. Saturday was free from regular work, as much as can be ascertained. On Saturday, the Lord's Supper, or a love feast, or a prayer meeting was held. Sunday offered a full round of worship throughout the day. Zinzendorf adhered to this weekend pattern, but he personally observed Saturday as a Sabbath of rest, a "practice until his end." Although Zinzendorf did not urge his opinion concerning the Sabbath rest upon any one, he did introduce it at the founding of the church, at the Bethlehem settlement in Pennsylvania, which became the headquarters for the North American Moravian mission program.[1]

John Wesley visited Herrnhut shortly after his conversion and commented: "I would gladly have spent my life here...Oh, when shall this Christianity cover the earth as the waters cover the sea."

John Wesley's Conversion

It is believed that Wesley adapted Moravian methods, but without doubt the Moravian Peter Boehler contributed to his conversion. It is strange that Wesley, an ordained minister of the Anglican church, did not understand that "by grace you are saved through faith" (Ephesians 2:8), and that Boehler had to tell him, "Preach faith till you have it." He finally acknowledged that "a true, living faith was the one thing needful" for him. Such faith in Christ, he learned, "is inseparable from a sense of pardon for all past, and freedom from all present sins." He was convinced, that he must renounce all dependence upon his "own works of righteousness," as practiced by following the letter of Christianity in his earlier Holy Club, and that he must trust wholly to the "Lamb of God that taketh away the sin of the world" (John 1:29). All of these thoughts coalesced at the Aldersgate Street prayer meeting of the Moravian Society in London, 1738, when he listened to the speaker reading Luther's preface to the Epistle to the Romans. This was his conversion related in his own words:

> While he was describing the change which God works in the heart through faith in Christ, I felt my heart strangely *warmed*. I felt I did trust in Christ, Christ alone for salvation: and an *assurance* was given me, that He had taken away my sins, even *mine*, and saved me from the law of sin and death.
>
> *John Wesley's Journal (Italics supplied)*

Can you, dear reader, relate to Wesley's experience, and be DRAWN TO CHRIST?

The Wesleyan Revival

After his conversion, Wesley's real work began in earnest. He preached in city after city all over England, Scotland, Ireland, and Wales, from pulpits when available, and in the open air to tens of thousands. His brother Charles, the songwriter, joined him, and so did George Whitefield and a host of lay preachers—and together they turned the world upside down for God. By 1791, when Wesley died, his followers numbered 79,000 in England, and 40,000 in America. Jonathan Edwards continued the spirit of Revival in New England with "deep convictions of sin, and transporting views of the excellency of Christ."[2]

Wesley's Preaching

Following Wesley's conversion, one would expect that the tenor of his preaching would be Christ and Him crucified (1 Corinthians 2:2), a lively faith in Christ leading to conversion, and a *practical Christian experience—the righteous fruits of salvation.* While Jonathan Edwards and George Whitefield held to Calvinistic predestination, Wesley was Armenian—thereby preaching an open, free gospel of salvation, with no strings of predestination attached. "The grace of God that bringeth salvation hath appeared to *all men*" (Titus 2:11). "Who will have all men to be saved, and to come unto the knowledge of the truth...who gave Himself a Ransom *for all*" (1 Timothy 2:3–6). Thus, Wesley preached Christ, as "the true light, which lighteth *every man* that cometh into the world" (John 1:9). (Italics supplied).

Wesley Upheld the Moral Law

The spiritual declension that had descended upon old England, just prior to the time of Wesley, was to a great degree the result of Antinomianism—teaching against the ten commandment law of God. Many affirmed that Christ had abolished the moral law, and that Christians are therefore under no obligation to observe it. Wesley cleared that notion by referring to Jesus statement: "Think not that I am come to destroy the law or the prophets: I am not come to destroy, but to fulfill" (Matthew 5:17). Wesley asserted: "the ritual or *ceremonial law*...our Lord indeed did come to destroy, to dissolve, and utterly abolish. But, the *moral law*, contained in the Ten Commandments, and enforced by the prophets, He did not take away. It was not the design of His coming to revoke any part of this. Every part of this law must remain in force upon all mankind, and in all ages."[3]

(Italics supplied)

Wesley extolled the law of God as: "a copy of the eternal Mind, a transcript of the Divine Nature." He declared three properties of the law of God as "Holy, Just and Good" (Romans 7:12). What is the function or use of the law? Wesley explained three distinct uses of the law.

Wesley Clear on: Law and the Gospel

The *first* use of the law, was taken from Romans, which reads: "I had not known sin, but by the law: for I had not known lust except the law had said, Thou shalt not covet" (Romans 7:7). The moral law is like a mirror (James 1:22–25) that reflects the condition of the heart, and as one looks into it, one sees "more and more of his own sinfulness," the transgression of the law actually defines sin (1 John 3:4). The first use of the law of God is that it convicts and condemns the sinner. Said Wesley: "The law flashes conviction on every side. He feels himself a mere sinner, and not until man is convicted of sin, will he truly feel his need of the atoning blood of Christ."[4]

Wesley's *second* use of the law centers on Galatians: "Wherefore the law was our schoolmaster to bring us unto Christ, that we might be justified by faith" (Galatians 3:24). After conviction of sin, the second use of the law, is that it drives, or brings us to Christ, where forgiveness takes place—washed in the atoning blood of the Lamb. The believer, having first come under the condemnation of the law, is driven by the law as a severe schoolmaster, to come under the grace of Christ (Romans 6:14) for cleansing from sin and salvation.

The *third* use of the law, Wesley explained, is to "keep us alive" or to keep us close to Christ, living out the principles of the law (John 14:15), as the natural *consequence of one's salvation*, obviously not the means of one's salvation. Wesley declared the perfect harmony of the law and the gospel so beautifully stated:

> There is, therefore, the closest connection that can be conceived between the law and the gospel. On the one hand, the law continually makes way for, and points us to the gospel; on the other, the gospel continually leads us to a more exact fulfilling of the law. The law, for instance, requires us to love God, to love our neighbor, to be meek, humble, or holy.[5]

THE GREAT REVIVAL ENDS ON A PROPHETIC NOTE

Wesley Anticipates End of Papal Dominance

Wesley was a great Champion of Christianity, preaching the pure gospel of salvation. He was also a champion of prophetic interpretation. He recognized the first beast of Revelation 13 as the: "Romish papacy." He believed the second beast (Revelation 13:11) was to arise "out of the earth"—out of Asia perhaps. Referring to the rise of the second beast in historical sequence, he said (1754), "But he is not yet come: though he cannot be far off. For he is to appear at the end of the forty two months of the first beast" (Revelation 13:5).[6]

End in Sight, of 1,260 Years Papal Dominance

The end of the 42 months would be 42 multiplied by 30, to give 1,260 days. Applying the *day for a year principle*, (Numbers 14:34; Ezekiel 4:6), that would mean 1,260 years dominance of the first beast, the Romish papacy—in which "power was given him to continue" (Revelation 13:5). This was the long-awaited culmination of papal power, related by the parallel prophecy of Daniel—in which "the saints shall be given into his hand" (Daniel 7:25).

The Romish papacy "shall persecute the saints of the Most High" (Daniel 7:25), who "fled into the wilderness, where she has a place prepared by God, that they should feed her there one thousand two hundred and sixty days" (Revelation 12:6).

Remember Drue Cressener (reference Chapter 6), was the *first* to date the 1,260 years of papal dominance from the Justinian era. Justinian's decree to *elevate* the pope as "universal head of the church," began in the year 538. Add 1,260 years, and we come up with 1798, at which time we look for the *deposition* of the pope, just the reverse of his *elevation*.

Papal Dominance Ends 1798

1798 marked the end of papal dominance—the end of persecution. Unconsciously the Baptists, champions for religious liberty, were led of God to bring about the Act of Toleration in England in 1689. Likewise, in America, Baptist appeals were loud and clear, culminating in the clauses relative to religious liberty in the Constitution of the United States, and in the Bill of Rights. Such guarantees spelled the doom to papal dominance and persecution by the year 1798.

Result of French Revolution: Collapse of Papal Power

But, there was an event of great significance that toppled the power of papal Rome—the French Revolution, 1789 to 1798. The atheistic Reign of Terror crushed the Roman church—churches were closed and desecrated abominably. The heads of nobles, ecclesiastics, and others, rolled from the guillotine, and the Bible was outlawed.

1798: Pope Deposed and Lost Papal States

To cap it all, in 1798, the French Directory dispatched General Berthier to march upon Rome and conquer it, to establish a Roman Republic. The Roman Republic was effected, which meant the Roman church was stripped of the possession of Rome, including much of the territory of the Papal States. Papal arms and insignia were removed. The Vatican Palace was pillaged, and the Swiss guards were replaced.

The finger of prophecy had pointed to 1798, and Pope Pius VI was *deposed* by General Berthier, to conclude the 1,260 years of papal dominance. The pope was banished from Rome, hurried from place to place, and exiled to Valence in southern France, where he expired, July, 1799.

Dissolution of Holy Roman Empire

The final stroke to destroy the power of papal Rome was the dissolution by Napoleon, in 1806, of the Holy Roman Empire, the political arm of the Roman papacy.

Even though, a new pope was elected in 1800, the crippled Papacy limped along thereafter, without the full possession of the *Papal States*, without the *Holy Roman Empire*, without ecclesiastical *revenue*, without *power*—a mere shadow of its former glory. But prophecy envisages a *resurgence* of papal power after its deathly blow—that is the subject of yet another book.

When the Roman Papacy had been crushed, and the pope was taken into captivity, a chorus of voices in England, Europe and America, gave a sigh of relief, as they witnessed the end of the 42 months, or 1,260 day-years of papal Rome (Revelation 13:5). And with the passing of the event of 1798, one of the clearest characteristics of prophecy was evident—that history is the true and final interpreter of prophecy, so that "when it come to pass, ye might believe" (John 14:29).

Significance of the Event of 1798

The year 1798 set mankind free from the shackles of ecclesiastical authority and superstition, to enter a new era of freedom from persecution, freedom of religion and conscience, and freedom of thought. And with the discovery of the Rosetta stone in 1799, the way was opened to authenticate the Bible and its prophecies, through the discoveries of Biblical archaeology. Thus, the *literal earth* "opened its mouth and swallowed up the flood" of fallacious teachings concerning the Bible (Revelation 12:16).

The year 1798, not only marked the end of the reign of papal tyranny, it marked the end of the existence of the "church in the wilderness." The metaphorical sun-clothed woman that fled into a wilderness experience, was subjected to papal dominance in one form or another, for 1,260 day-years (Revelation 12:6,14).

Whole masses of Christians comprised the church in the wilderness: Waldenses, Lollards, Hussites, the Protestant Reformation, French Huguenots, true Anabaptists, Baptists and Seventh Day Baptists, Pietists, the Moravians, the Wesleyans, and any others during that period, that kept close to the Scriptures and away from Rome.

After 1798, there emerges a *new phase* of the TRUE CHURCH that has come out of the *wilderness phase* of 1,260 years. It is the last, and final phase of the church, described in the last verse of Revelation 12, at verse 17 as follows:

> And the dragon was enraged with the woman, and he went to make war with the rest of her offspring, who keep the commandments of God and have the testimony of Jesus Christ.
>
> *The New King James Version*

Irrespective of denominational lines, we are confronted with Christ's invisible church, that emerged after 1798, and will continue to the end of time, whose lines of demarcation are: the observance of the commandments of God and having the testimony of Jesus Christ.

Friend, you and I are confronted with Christ's TRUE CHURCH of the last days, of vital interest to *all mankind*. Let's dip into the next chapter in great anticipation, as Champions of Christianity in search of TRUTH.

(9)

LAST DAY CHURCH AND THE TESTIMONY OF JESUS

> And the dragon was enraged with the woman, and he went to make war with the rest of her offspring, who keep the commandments of God and have the testimony of Jesus Christ (Revelation 12:17).
>
> *The New King James Version*

The church that emerges after 1798, concluding the 1,260 years in the wilderness, is designated as "the rest of her offspring." This is the TRUE CHURCH of the metaphorical sun-clothed woman of Revelation chapter twelve—the simplest graphic portrayal of the entire history of the Christian Church. This is the church that is left over, the LAST DAY CHURCH.

The identifying marks of the last day church, is that it observes the commandments of God—the ten commandments. Second, the church has or "holds to the TESTIMONY OF JESUS' (New International Version Revelation 12:17; Capitalization supplied).

Revelation fourteen describes the last day church as "those who keep the commandments of God and the faith of Jesus" (verse 12). Verse four says: "These are the ones who follow the Lamb wherever He goes."

We roundup Revelation's description of the last day church—they follow the Lamb very closely, they hold to the faith of Jesus, and hold to the testimony of Jesus. They have responded to Jesus' Great Commission: "Go therefore and make disciples of all nations, baptizing them in the name of the Father and of the Son and of the Holy Spirit, teaching them *to observe all things that I have commanded you*; and lo I am with you always, even to the end of the age" (New King James Matthew 28:19,20; Italics supplied).

The last day church holds to the testimony of Jesus, which means they "observe all things" that Jesus has commanded, taught and related. They observe and follow the Lamb very closely.

I don't think we can cover in this book, the observance of all things that Jesus commanded or taught, but we can cover some major teachings of Jesus, that are absolutely essential. The teachings of Jesus are not designed to tickle the fancy of the hearers, but are to become part and parcel of one's personal experience—to be "observed" and carried out in practice.

The greatest *testimony* ,or teaching that Jesus commanded, was on the matter of Salvation,and here follow some texts (quoted from the New King James Version for this Chapter).

TESTIMONY OF JESUS ON SALVATION

"For God so loved the world that He gave His only begotten Son, that whoever believes in Him should not perish but have everlasting life" (John 3:16).

In answer to the jailer who asked, "What must I do to be saved?" Paul replied, "Believe on the Lord Jesus Christ, and you will be saved" (Acts 16:30,31). To believe in Jesus, is first of all to believe that Jesus really exists, that He is the historic figure described in the Bible. Second, one must extend that belief, to include what the eunuch confessed to Philip, "I believe that Jesus Christ is the Son of God" (Acts 8:37). That means Jesus is more than a human historic figure—He is human-divine, "Immanuel, which is translated God with us" (Matthew 1:23). Third, to believe in Jesus means to believe in, and to appropriate His sacrificial death on the cross for one's sins. "Behold! the Lamb of God who takes away the sin of the world" (John 1:29). Peter describes how salvation is transacted on the cross, where Jesus takes the punishment of death (Romans 6:23) for man's sins: "Who Himself bore our sins in His own body on the tree, that we, having died to sins, might live for righteousness—by whose stripes we are healed" (1 Peter 2:24).

"You shall call His name Jesus, for He will save His people from their sins" (Matthew 1:21). Notice, that Jesus does not save people *in* their sins, but *from* their sins. Furthermore, He does not promptly take away our sins, without us doing something about them—"having died to sins," as Peter said. The way to die to sins is explained in Acts, Chapter two:

> v. 36. Therefore let all the house of Israel know assuredly that God has made this Jesus, whom you crucified, both Lord and Christ.
>
> v. 37. Now when they heard this, they were cut to the heart, and said to Peter and the rest of the apostles, Men and brethren what shall we do?
>
> v. 38. Then Peter said to them *repent*, and let every one of you be baptized in the name of Jesus Christ for the *remission of sins*; and you shall receive the gift of the Holy Spirit.

The New King James Version (Italics supplied).

After hearing about Jesus, the Israelite crowd was convinced, their consciences were awakened, they were aware of the awfulness of their sins, and they cried out what shall we do? As quick as a flash, Peter told them what to do, and that was to *repent*. Repentance includes sorrow for sins, and a turning away from them. It also includes confession of sins for remission from the hand of God. When these things are effected salvation is complete. "Having died to sin," said Peter, Jesus has saved from sins (Matthew 1:21), and has taken them away (John 1:29) to Calvary's Cross. Then "we, having died to sins, might live for righteousness—by whose stripes we are healed" (1 Peter 2:24).

> How sweet the name of Jesus sounds
> In a believer's ear!
> Amazing grace! How sweet the sound—
> That saved a wretch like me!

Then Jesus said to His disciples:

> If anyone desires to come after Me, let him deny
> himself, and take up his cross, and follow Me.
> 'For whoever desires to save his life will lose it,
> and whoever loses his life for My sake will find it.
> 'For what is a man profited if he gains the whole
> world, and loses his own soul?
> Or what will a man give in exchange for his soul'?

Matthew 16:24–26

> 'And I, if I be lifted up from the earth,
> will draw all peoples to Myself.'

John 12:32
The New King James Version

Have you, noble reader, been DRAWN TO CHRIST—have you felt the magnetic pull of the cross? "Believe on the Lord Jesus Christ, and you will be saved" (Acts 16:31).

TESTIMONY OF JESUS ON THE TEN COMMANDMENTS

Under the subject of Salvation, we learned that the Son of God was to be named "Jesus, for He will save His people from their sins" (Matthew 1:21). To be saved from our sins we must repent, and confess them, as John reminds us in his epistle: "If we confess our sins, He is faithful and just to forgive us our sins and to cleanse us from all unrighteousness" (1 John 1:9).

But, the big question is—what is sin? What constitutes sin, and how can we define it? Well let's allow the Holy Scriptures to define sin. John's epistle can help us: "For sin is the transgression of the law" (1 John 3:4). Paul adds: "For by the law is the knowledge of sin" (Romans 3:20). Paul again fortifies the definition of sin: "I would not have known sin except through the law. For I would not have known covetousness unless the law had said, "You shall not covet" (Romans 7:7).

These verses are all from the New Testament, demonstrating the continuity of the ten commandments in New Testament times. But, we all understand the commandments were written on tables of stone by God, and presented to Israel by Moses at Mount Sinai in Old Testament times. We may not be aware of the fact that the ten precepts were known before Mount Sinai. A good illustration of that is the experience of Joseph, in which the transgression, or breaking of any commandment of the ten, constituted sin. Joseph was sensitive to sin, for when his master's wife tempted him to commit adultery, by breaking the seventh commandment "he refused and said to his master's wife.... How then can I do this great wickedness, and *sin against God*?" (Genesis 39:7–10; Italics supplied).

From the foregoing it is crystal clear, that sin is the transgression, or breaking of any one, or more of the ten commandments. The continued, willful breaking of the commandments will keep us out of heaven. Therefore, the conscientious believer repents of his sins, and turns away from them. Instead of trampling upon the commandments, he naturally upholds them, and through faith "establishes the law" (Romans 3:31), and receives the commendation of Jesus: "whoever does and teaches them, he shall be called great in the kingdom of heaven" (Matthew 5:19). John in the closing chapter of the Bible pronounces a blessing on those who love God's "commandments more than gold": "Blessed are those that do His commandments, that they may have right to the tree of life, and may enter through the gates into the city" (Revelation 22:14). On the other hand, notice those who are left out of the city New Jerusalem, the City of God in the next verse, and please count the number of commandments they are breaking. "But *outside* are dogs and *sorcerers and sexually immoral* and *murderers and idolaters*, and whoever loves and practices a lie" (Revelation 22:15; Italics supplied).

Friend, do you love Jesus? Do you really? Remember, that question was put to Peter three times (John 21:15–17). Can you reply like Zinzendorf: "I have one passion, tis He!" Well then, you'll have no problem with what Jesus said as one of the greatest testimonies of Jesus, "If you love me, keep my commandments" (John 14:15). Take hold of this *testimony of Jesus*, for it is a mark of the last day church.

We demonstrate our love for Jesus, when we observe His commandments, and it brings us into a closer relationship, to really know Him as a God of love. "Now by this we know that we know Him, if we keep His commandments. He who says, 'I *know* Him,' and does not keep His commandments is a liar and the *truth* is not in him" (1 John 2:3,4; Italics supplied). John is so full of the law of love that he writes further: "By this we know that we love the children of God, when we love God, and keep His commandments. For this is the love of God, that we keep His commandments. And His commandments are not burdensome" (1 John 5:2,3).

Someone has said, are there not two commandments, instead of ten? That is (1) to love God supremely, and (2) to love one's neighbor as himself. Absolutely right, but Jesus taught, "On these two commandments hang all the Law and the Prophets" (Matthew 22:40). On these two commandments hang, or are derived all ten commandments, just as the ten fingers on two hands, hang on two arms. A cursory reading of the ten commandments in Exodus 20, verses

3 to 17, reveals the first four commandments are love to God, the next six commandments are love to our fellow-men. Writing with special emphasis on love toward our fellow-men Paul summarizes: "Owe no one anything except to love one another, for he who loves another has fulfilled the law. For the commandments, You shall not commit adultery, You shall not murder, You shall not steal, You shall not bear false witness, You shall not covet, and if there is any other commandment, are all summed up in this saying, namely, You shall love your neighbor as yourself. Love does no harm to a neighbor; therefore love is the fulfillment of the law" (Romans 13:8–10; See also Galatians 5:14).

TESTIMONY OF JESUS ON THE SABBATH COMMANDMENT

In the New Testament emphasis is given to the commandment of love toward our neighbors, and is sometimes spelled out in the six commandments. The first four commandments are not spelled out, but that does not mean they are abrogated. They are generally summarized in love toward God. Nevertheless, in love toward God, the first four commandments are implied. The fourth commandment requires attention, equal to the other nine. Therefore the breaking of the fourth commandment constitutes *sin*, equal to the breaking of any of the other nine. So, this is serious business, in the matter of salvation from "sin and death" (Romans 8:2). Strangely enough, details of the fourth commandment are spelled out more than any of the others, and here it is for our attention from Exodus, Chapter 20:

> v. 8. Remember the Sabbath day, to keep it holy.
>
> v. 9. Six days you shall labor and do all your work,
>
> v.10. but the seventh day is the Sabbath of the Lord your God. In it you shall do no work: you, nor your son, nor your daughter, nor your manservant, nor your maidservant, nor your cattle, nor your stranger who is within your gates.
>
> v.11. For in six days the Lord made the heavens and the earth, the sea, and all that is in them, and rested the seventh day. Therefore the Lord blessed the Sabbath day and hallowed it.

The New King James Version

Such was the fourth commandment given at Mount Sinai, along with the other nine. But, the commandment itself indicates the *origin* of the Sabbath, For or because "in six days the Lord made heaven and earth...and rested the seventh day" (verse 11).

The Sabbath was instituted at creation as the seventh day (Genesis 2:1–3), immediately after creation in six literal days, comprising darkness and light, like the days at the present time (Genesis 1:5,31). The fact that the first Sabbath was kept by Adam and Eve in the Garden of Eden, nullifies the charge that the

Sabbath is Jewish. Adam was not a Jew, he predates the existence of the Jewish nation by a couple thousand years, or more. Jesus himself confirmed that point, when He declared: "The Sabbath was made for man" (Mark 2:27). That is man, or mankind in the generic sense, and Adam is the father of mankind—the human race. If the Sabbath was made for the Jew, Jesus would have said so accordingly, but He didn't.

The commandment itself indicates another important point, and that is the *seventh day* is designated the "Sabbath of the Lord" (verse 10). If it is the Sabbath of the Lord—then it is the Lord's Day. Jesus also confirmed that, when he stated: "Therefore the Son of Man is also Lord of the Sabbath" (Mark 2:28). If Jesus is the Lord of the Sabbath—then it is the Lord's Day.

Twice the commandment says *the seventh day*. That means the specific seventh day at the end of the weekly cycle, was set in motion by God Himself, and *guided by His hand*. There is no other phenomenon to guide the weekly cycle, unlike the rotation of the earth on its axis every 24 hours, or the motion of the earth around the sun in 365¼ days. The specificity of *the seventh day* as the Sabbath, rules out the one-in-seven selection, or the choice of any seventh day running through the week—which only makes for chaos, and God is a God of order.

About fifteen hundred years after the presentation of the commandments at Sinai, we come across a few Christian women, who had no difficulty in locating the Sabbath at the end of the weekly cycle. With touching pathos Luke describes the death and burial of Christ. After Jesus' death on the cross (Luke 23:46), he mentions Joseph of Arimathea withdrawing Jesus' body from the cross, and placing it in his own new tomb in the rock, and records: "That day was the Preparation, and the Sabbath drew on" (Luke 23:54). All Christendom acknowledges the death of Christ on "Good Friday," and that day is called the Preparation—the customary physical and mental preparation for the holy Sabbath that "drew on," or followed Friday. Since Saturday follows Friday, Saturday is the Sabbath, and still is the seventh day at the end of the week. And the rest of the story goes on in Luke's own words:

> And the women who had come with Him from Galilee followed after, and they observed the tomb and how His body was laid.
>
> Then they returned and prepared spices and fragrant oils. And they *rested on the Sabbath according to the commandment.*
>
> *Luke 23:55,56. (Italics supplied)*
> *The New King James Version*

After the necessary, hurried preparation, late Friday afternoon, these faithful female disciples of Christ, did not even place their love gift, a fragrant preparation, on Christ's body on the Sabbath. Instead, they rested entirely, according to the details of the commandment, given about fifteen hundred years before their day, and without any equivocation of the identity of the true Sabbath day. Only on the first day of the week, namely, Sunday, did they go to Christ's tomb, bearing their fragrant preparation at the break of day (Luke 24:1). Oh, if only twentieth century Christians would follow the example of those faithful women!

That's right, the Sabbath was not just for Christians in Christ's day. It is for all generations, for all time. And Jesus made that clear, when, with reference to the forthcoming destruction of Jerusalem in A.D. 70 by the Romans under Titus, He warned: "Pray that your flight may not be in winter or on the Sabbath" (Matthew 24:20).

Jesus uttered those words a good forty years before the destruction of Jerusalem, thereby implying the Sabbath would still be observed forty years hence. And if forty years hence, why not thereafter, for all time? Jesus gave no indication of limitation, or cessation of the Sabbath. And as the story goes, the Christians carried out their flight to safety, before the destruction of Jerusalem, true to the words of Jesus. The Jewish historian Graetz records their *flight* before the onslaught of winter, in the beginning of the month of October, and on a Wednesday, making way for them to observe the Sabbath without anxiety."[1]

By the way, obedience to the fourth commandment is a strong motivation for observing the Sabbath. But, stronger still is the motivation to follow the example of Christ: "So He came to Nazareth, where He had been brought up. And as His custom was, He went into the synagogue on the Sabbath day, and stood up for to read" (Luke 4:16). A Christian may be defined as one who follows Christ—right! So let's follow Him in His observance of the Sabbath. The Ethiopian ambassador to the court of Lisbon in 1534, stated his reasons for keeping the Sabbath, "But in obedience to Christ and His Holy apostles, that we observe that day."[2]

TESTIMONY OF JESUS ON BAPTISM BY IMMERSION

John the Baptist "was baptizing in Aenon, near Salim, because there was *much water* there. And they came and were baptized" (John 3:23; Italics supplied). John also baptized in the Jordan river, and Matthew gives the historic account:

> Then Jesus when He had been baptized,
> *came up immediately from the water*;
> and behold, the heavens were opened to Him,
> And He saw the Spirit of God
> descending like a dove and alighting upon Him,
> And suddenly a voice came from heaven,
> saying, 'This is My Beloved Son, in whom
> I am well pleased.'

Matthew 3:16,17 (Italics supplied)
The New King James Version

Jesus didn't need to be baptized, since He was sinless, and did not need salvation. But, He set an example for us to follow, and more than that, baptism is a testimony of Jesus, better still a command (Matthew 28:19), a *must*:

> Jesus answered, 'Most assuredly, I say to you,
> unless one is born of water and the Spirit,
> he cannot enter the kingdom of God.
> Do not marvel that I said to you,
> You *must* be born again.'

John 3:5,7 (Italics supplied)
The New King James Version

Baptism is the climax or consummation of one's Christian experience. The ritual of baptism in water is a public testimony of the inner regeneration, turn around, new birth, brought about through the power of the Holy Spirit.

As already noted in the introduction to the subject of baptism, there is to be "much water" (John 3:23), so that the candidate can be fully immersed, and then come up from the water as did Jesus (Matthew 3:16,17). The other modes of baptism, sprinkling and pouring, vacate the ordinance of its meaning, and render the significance of the rite senseless. Only immersion (signified by the Greek *baptisma*), submersion, and emergence can rightly symbolize the death, burial, and resurrection of Christ.

Going through the motion of baptism avails nothing, if there has not been an inner rebirth wrought by the Holy Spirit. Paul furnishes us with an excellent passage of Scripture on the subject:

> Therefore we were buried with Him through baptism into death, that just as Christ was raised from the dead by the glory of the Father, even so we also should *walk in newness of life*. Knowing this that our old man was crucified with Him, that the body of sin might be done away with, that we should no longer be slaves to sin.

Romans 6:4,6 (Italics supplied)
The New King James Version

The candidate for baptism identifies himself with the three great events of Christ. The candidate's baptism is a memorial of the (1) death, (2) burial and (3) resurrection of Christ. More importantly, baptism applied to the believer means:

(1) Christ's death really must become the believer's death to sin—no longer a slave to sin.

(2) Christ's burial really must become the believer's burial of the "old" life of sin (Infants cannot be baptized, because they do not have an "old man" of sin).

(3) Christ's resurrection really must become the believer's resurrection to "walk in newness of life."

In baptism salvation is consummated, as Mark remarks: "He who believes and is baptized will be saved; but he who does not believe will be condemned" (Mark 16:16). Baptism has depth of meaning, and when it is entered into with heartfelt preparation, the blessing of baptism is bountiful. Baptism is no snap decision. There are steps to be taken before baptism, in preparation for the greatest event to an individual, like a second birthday—being born again spiritually. Here is an outline of preparation for baptism:

(1) Baptism requires belief: Mark 16:16; Acts 8:37.

(2) Baptism requires repentance: Acts 2:38.

(3) Baptism requires instruction: "teaching them to observe all things that I have commanded you" (Matthew 28:20).

(4) Baptism requires that the believer reflects the "new creation; old things have passed away; behold, all things have become new" (2 Corinthians 5:17).

Baptism is the climax of a holy and solemn union between the individual Christian and Christ. "For as many of you as were baptized into Christ have PUT ON CHRIST" (Galatians 3:27; Capitalization supplied). That is the closest that one can be DRAWN TO CHRIST.

"And now why are *you waiting*? Arise and be baptized, and wash away your sins, calling on the name of the Lord" (Acts 22:16; Italics supplied).

O now I see the crimson wave
The fountain deep and wide,
Jesus, my Lord, mighty to save
Points to His wounded side.

—*Mrs. Phoebe Palmer*

TESTIMONY OF JESUS ON THE SLEEP OF DEATH

To solve the riddle of the state of man in death we consider the creation of Adam: "And the Lord God formed man of the dust of the ground, and breathed into his nostrils the *breath of life*; and man became a living being" (Genesis 2:7; Italics supplied). Reduced to the simplest formula it would read:

BODY PLUS BREATH OF LIFE = LIVING BEING

The breath of life is God's way of describing the essence of life—unseen, and without shape or form, indefinable. Job discusses the essence of life: "All the while my *breath* is in me, and the *Spirit* of God is in my nostrils (Job 27:3; Italics supplied). Adam had the breath in his nostrils, Job had the Spirit in his nostrils. Hence breath and spirit are synonymous. Would it surprise you to discover that the same essence of life is in the animals:

> For what happens to the sons of men also happens to beasts; one thing befalls them: as one dies so dies the other. Surely, they *all have one breath*; man has no advantage over beasts, for all is vanity. All go to one place: all are from the dust, and all return to dust (Ecclesiastes 3:19,20; Italics supplied)
>
> *The New King James Version*

When it comes to the essence of life, the whole live creation is sustained by *one breath*, whether man or beast. All die the same way, and we do not go immediately upon death to either heaven or hell, but to one place—the dust of the earth. Thus, our formula for the creation of life is reversed in death. Therefore, death is the *reverse of creation*, reduced to the simplest formula it reads:

BODY MINUS BREATH OF LIFE = DEAD PERSON

At death the body disintegrates, decomposes, and returns to dust, and Solomon describes what happens to the breath of life, or the spirit, or simply the essence of life: "Then the dust will return to the earth as it was, and the spirit will return to God who gave it" (Ecclesiastes 12:7).

The essence of life belongs to God, but it has no existence, personality, or form apart from the body. David fills out the picture: "His breath goeth forth, he returneth to his earth; in that very day his thoughts perish" (A.V. Psalms 146:4). As soon as one dies the thoughts perish—there is no conscious entity that survives death, that can think, act, or do anything apart from the body. There is only life upon *union* of the body and the essence of life.

More than fifty times in the Bible death is likened to sleep. Sleep is a state of unconsciousness, in which one is oblivious to one's surroundings, oblivious to the passing of time or events. David spoke of the "sleep of death" (Psalms 13:3), which is total unconsciousness—extinction. And David, along with all the dead are in that state. Observe Luke's comments on David: "Let me speak freely to you of the patriarch David, that he is both dead and buried, and his tomb is with us to this day. For David *did not ascend into the heavens*" (Acts 2:29,34; Italics supplied).

How long does a person remain in the sleep of death? Answer: until the Resurrection. Even at the time of Christ's resurrection a number were raised—re-created in body, complete with the breath of life. I'll let Matthew tell the gripping story: "And the *graves were opened*; and many *bodies* of the saints who had fallen asleep were raised; and coming out of the graves after His resurrection, they went into the holy city and appeared to many" (Matthew 27:52,53; Italics supplied).

What a glorious day that was, and after that, when Jesus ascended to heaven the resurrected saints accompanied Him. Paul relates that wonderful, climactic event: "When He ascended up on high, He led a multitude of captives, and gave gifts unto men" (A.V. Ephesians 4:8). The multitude of captives were those that had been captives of the grave, now they were his captives with eternal life.

We note the Resurrection of Christ with the group of saints, but there is to be a Resurrection at the end of time. Job was looking forward to that resurrection when he wrote: "So man lies down and does not rise. Till the heavens are no more, they will not *awake* nor be roused out of their *sleep*" (Job 14:12; Italics supplied; See also Daniel 12:2).

The last day church needs the Testimony of Jesus to confirm the sleep of death, and here it is from the Gospel of John:

> These things He said, and after that
> He said to them 'Our friend Lazarus *sleeps*,
> but I go that I may *wake him up*.'
> Then His disciples said, 'Lord, if he sleeps
> he will get well'
> However, Jesus spoke of his *death*,
> but they thought that He was speaking about taking
> rest in sleep.
> Then Jesus said to them plainly, 'Lazarus is
> *dead*.'

John 11:11–14 (Italics supplied).
The New King James Version

Before Jesus miraculously raised Lazarus from the dead, He assured Martha of the future Grand Resurrection to take place at His Second Coming. He said, "Your brother will rise again." Martha made her testimony clear, "I know that he will *rise again in the resurrection at the last day*" (John 11:23,24; Italics supplied). May that also be your testimony!

TESTIMONY OF JESUS ON GOD'S STRANGE ACT

The Testimony of Jesus on Salvation is contained in the most-loved text in Scripture, but I am sure Christians are not aware that this text is a Testimony of God's strange act. Let's repeat it together: "For God so loved the world that He gave His only begotten Son, that whoever believes in Him should not *perish* but have everlasting life" (John 3:16; Italics supplied). Those who believe will have everlasting life. Those who do not believe will not have everlasting life in a fiery hell, they will have the opposite of life—they will PERISH. To perish means total destruction, or annihilation.

The current belief is that at death, the wicked go to hell, where they continually burn throughout the ceaseless ages of eternity, as *disembodied spirits*. Jesus puts this belief to rest in just one sentence. Here comes Jesus most poignant testimony on hell: "Fear Him who is able to destroy both soul and body in hell" (Matthew 10:28). In the first place this text says the wicked are DESTROYED, they do not live continually in Hell. Second, the wicked are *not disembodied spirits in hell*. Hell fire destroys *both soul (life) and body*. Third, mankind does not possess an immortal soul, since it is destroyed in hell.

It is the view of many that hell is burning now, but the location of hell is somewhat nebulous. The Bible answers the "when" and "where" of hell. Jesus tells us hell takes place at the end of the world: "The tares are gathered and *burned* in the fire, so it will be at the *end of the world*" (Matthew 13:40; Italics supplied).

Where on earth is hell? Good question! Hell is on earth at the close of the millennium. "They went up on the breadth of the earth.... And fire came down from God out of heaven and *devoured* them. Then death and hades were cast into the lake of fire. This is the *second death*. And anyone not found in the Book of Life was cast into the lake of fire" (Revelation 20:9,14,15; Italics supplied). There is no one living ceaselessly in fiery torments. The wicked are devoured, it is the second death.

Peter paints a graphic picture in 2 Peter, Chapter 3, of the inferno on earth in which "the elements will melt with fervent heat; both the earth and the works that are in it will be *burned up*." Peter says that the atmospheric heavens and the existing earth is "reserved for fire until the day of judgment and *perdition of ungodly men*." The greatest conflagration of all time will destroy the earth and its wicked inhabitants, and the fire will go out, to make way for a new earth. "Nevertheless we, according to His promise look for new heavens and a *new earth* in which righteousness dwells." (Italics supplied).

Jesus uses the term "everlasting fire" when talking about hell (Matthew 25:41). What is meant, is that the fire is not everlasting in its burning, but in its *results*. Jude also uses the term "eternal fire" that destroyed Sodom and Gomorrah (Jude 7). We are aware of the fact that these cities are not still burning eternally, but the *results* of the burned out cities are *eternal*.

Peter elaborates on the results of Divine fire that burned up the cities, and sets them forth as an example of the future destruction of the ungodly. "And turning the cities of Sodom and Gomorrah into *ashes*, condemned them to *destruction*, making them an example to those who afterward would live ungodly" (2 Peter 2:6; Italics supplied). Malachi says the wicked will be "burned up" and reduced to "ashes" (Malachi 4:1–3).

God does not gloat over the destruction of the wicked. The Scriptures do not show a God, more tyrannical than any human despot, torturing His wicked created beings ceaselessly in the flames of hell. And to what purpose would God want to keep the wicked burning—only to perpetuate sin and sinners? No! God "will make an utter end of it. Affliction will not rise up a second time"

(Nahum 1:9). God "will bring to pass His act, His strange act" (A.V. Isaiah 28:21), in the annihilation of the wicked, described by Ezekiel, "I have no pleasure in the death of the wicked, but that the wicked turn from his way and live. Turn, turn from your evil ways! For why should you die?" (Ezekiel 33:11).

TESTIMONY OF JESUS ON THE SECOND ADVENT

"The moment a man takes hold of the truth that Jesus Christ is coming back again...this world loses its hold upon him." I'm sure you agree with this testimony of the famous evangelist Dwight L. Moody. listen to the testimony of Jesus on His Second Coming:

> Let not your heart be troubled; you believe in God,
> believe also in Me.
> In My Father's house are many mansions;
> if it were not so I would have told you.
> I go to prepare a place for you.
> And if I go and prepare a place for you
> I will come again and receive you to Myself;
> that where I am there you may be also.

John 14:1–3
The New King James Version

During the first century of the Christian era Jesus made the promise—"I will come again." And here we are in the twentieth century, and Jesus has not come back yet. How will we know when He will come? He tells us, that when the fig tree begins to put forth leaves, we know that summer is near, "So you also, when you see these things, know that it is near, at the very doors" (Matthew 24:33).

The expression "when you see these things" refers to the ten-point prophecy of Matthew, Chapter twenty four, in which Jesus outlines prophecies, as signs in the skies and on earth, to be fulfilled before Jesus returns. Without going into a dissertation of these signs, I believe we are living in the season for the Second Coming to take place.

May I suggest, dear reader, that you study these signs, to come to the same conviction. For good measure, I'll pick one such sign: "For nation shall rise against nation and kingdom against kingdom" (Matthew 24:7). Never before, in the history of warfare were so many nations and kingdoms involved, as in World War I and II. Such proportions of involvement and escalation on a worldwide scale suggests fulfillment of this prophecy. That means Christ could return before too long, surely before the close of the twenty first century!

Besides giving the signs before the Second Advent, Matthew twenty four also describes the manner of Christ's coming—the event itself. There is nothing secret about the Second Coming: "For as the lightning comes from the east and flashes to the west, so also will the coming of the Son of Man be" (Matthew 24:27). The Second Coming is visible—it fills the skies. Matthew continues: "Then the sign of the Son of Man will appear in heaven, and then all the tribes of the earth will mourn, and they will *see* the Son of Man coming on the clouds of heaven with power and great glory. And He will send His angels with a great *sound* of a trumpet, and they will gather His elect from the four winds, from one end of the heaven to the other" (Matthew 24:30.31; Italics supplied).

We glean important points from this description, that the event is *visible to all*, including the wicked. It is *audible*—from the sound of the trumpet. The Second Coming is designed to reap the harvest of the elect. The Second Coming will separate the wheat from the tares, the sheep from the goats (Matthew 13:36–43; 25:31–46).

The harvest of the elect is made up of two groups: (1) those who are in the "sleep" of death (1 Thessalonians 4:15), the dead Christians, who are resurrected; (2) those Christians who are alive at the Second Advent, who are translated without dying.

I'll let Paul speak: "For the Lord Himself will descend from heaven with a *shout*, with the voice of an archangel, and with the trumpet of God. And the *dead in Christ will rise first*. Then we who are alive and remain shall be caught up together with them in the clouds to *meet* the Lord in the air. And thus we shall always be with the Lord" (1 Thessalonians 4:16,17; Italics supplied).

Once again we are confronted with a tumultuous Second Advent, nothing secretive or hidden. Even Jesus does not appear as a phantom, it is the "Lord himself" in person, "this *same* Jesus who was taken up from you into heaven, will so come *in like manner* as you saw Him go into heaven" (Acts 1:11; Italics supplied). John says, "Every eye will see Him" (Revelation 1:7). Paul concludes the passage under study, saying the two groups of the saved meet the Lord in the air, to always be "with the Lord," as He takes them to heaven. Note that it is *only* at the Second Advent that we shall be "with the Lord"—not at any time *before*. In other words, when a person dies, he is not "with the Lord" upon death—that only happens at the Second Advent.

And where do you and I come into the picture? Paul tells us: "I have fought a good fight, I have finished the race, I have kept the faith. Finally, there is laid up for me the crown of righteousness, which the Lord, the righteous Judge, will give to me on that Day, and not to me only but also to all those who have *loved His appearing*" (2 Timothy 4:7,8; Italics supplied).

TESTIMONY OF JESUS ON CHRISTIAN STEWARDSHIP

I believe there is a sin that we are afraid to mention. Now, we know that it is a sin to rob our neighbor, but isn't it a sin if we rob God? Here it comes from Malachi: "Will a man rob God? Yet you have robbed Me! But you say, 'In what way have we robbed You?" In *tithes and offerings*" (Malachi 3:8; Italics supplied).

Well! Giving tithe? That is a tenth of one's income. It is an old Jewish custom, that has died out. Wrong! It is not a Jewish custom. Right! It has died out.

Actually, tithing goes back to Abraham, before the Jewish nation. He gave tithe to Melchizedek, the first known priest of God Most High who said: "Blessed be Abram of God Most High, Possessor of heaven and earth.... And he gave him a tithe of all" (Genesis 14:18–20).

Several times in the book of Hebrews, in the New Testament, Jesus Christ is called a "priest for ever according to the order of Melchizedek" (Hebrews 5:6). That being the case, then, Jesus has the right to receive tithe like Melchizedek did. In fact, he encouraged the rendering of tithe. Here is the testimony of Jesus on Christian stewardship. "But woe to you Pharisees! For you tithe mint and rue and all manner of herbs, and pass by justice and the love of God. These you ought to have done, without leaving the other undone." (Luke 11:42; See also Matthew 23:23). Both the love of God and the rendering of tithe, Jesus taught, should ride in tandem.

After the priest Melchizedek, God appointed the tribe of Levi to serve Israel as priests. The Levitical priesthood was hereditary, and they received the tithe for their service in the tabernacle. It was for their upkeep and support. Moses wrote: "I have given the children of Levi all the tithes in Israel as an inheritance in return for the work which they perform, the work of the tabernacle of meeting" (Numbers 18:21).

With regard to the New Testament era, Paul draws parallels from the Old Testament era, for the support of the gospel ministry: "Do you not know that those who minister the holy things eat of the things of the temple, and those who serve at the altar partake of the offerings of the altar? *Even so the Lord has commanded that those who preach the gospel should live from the gospel*" (1 Corinthians 9:13,14; Italics supplied).

The Christian recognizes God's ownership of all, so that the rendering of tithe for the support of the ministry of the gospel is no burden to him. And after all it demonstrates his love for the gospel ministry, and God loves a cheerful giver. On top of it all, God blesses the faithful steward—so well expressed by Malachi:

> 'Bring all the tithes into the storehouse [church
> treasury], That there may be food in My house,
> And prove Me now in this'
> Says the Lord of hosts,
> 'If I will not open for you the windows of heaven
> And pour out for you such a blessing
> That there will not be room enough to receive it.

And I will *rebuke the devourer* for your sakes,
So that he will not destroy the fruit of your
ground."

Malachi 3:10, 11 (Italics supplied)
The New King James Version

TESTIMONY OF JESUS ON CHRISTIAN ORDINANCES

Foot-Washing

If we are going to adhere to Christ's Great Commission, "to observe all things that I have commanded you" (Matthew 28:20), then the Ordinance of Foot-Washing is an imperative. The testimony of Jesus on foot-washing is a clear mandate, equal in importance to the Lord's Supper. John writes:

If I then your Lord and Teacher, have washed your
feet, you also *ought* to wash one another's feet.
For I have given you an *example*,
that you should do as I have done to you.
Most assuredly, I say to you, a servant is
not greater than his master; nor is he who
is sent greater than he who sent him.
If you know these things, happy are you
if you *do them*.

John 13:14–17 (Italics supplied)
The New King James Version

For the individual believer the significance of foot-washing is likened to a *miniature baptism*. The believer has been washed entirely from sin by baptism. But, there is need for the washing of the feet, denoting a partial cleansing from occasional sins that have accumulated, like dust soiling the feet (John 13:10).

The ordinance does not imply washing one's own feet, but "washing one another's feet" (John 13:14). The believer selects a partner, and each person in turn washes the other's feet, by dipping the feet in a basin of water, and thereafter drying the feet with a hand towel. The significance of the act is that *pride* is rebuked. One has stooped to wash another's feet, as an act of *humility, equality, and service*.

The foot-washing ceremony is an ordinance of reconciliation. If a person in the church has hurt or offended another, this is an opportunity for reconciliation. He may invite the offended person to participate as his partner in foot-washing. As he washes the feet of the offended, *a bond of love and reconciliation* is formed. Fellowship and love is fully restored, ill-feelings and offenses are washed away. Thus, the two brothers have been prepared for the sacramental service of the Lord's Supper.

Lord's Supper

The foot-washing ordinance is carried out by believers pairing off by gender, into separate rooms, set up for the ordinance. At the conclusion of the ordinance, believers enter the sanctuary to celebrate the Lord's Supper. Therefore, the foot-washing ordinance is attached to the Lord's Supper, and as a preparatory service, it adds more significance to the Lord's Supper.

The key thought of the celebration of the Lord's Supper is that it is *commemorative*. It is a *memorial* to be celebrated: "This do in remembrance of Me" (1 Corinthians 11:24).

None of the texts on the Lord's Supper suggest any exclusiveness. All who wish may partake of the ordinance—both the "bread" and the "fruit of the vine." These two symbols are not to be separated, they belong together and are available to all who desire to participate (Mark 14:23). No one is excluded.

An interesting observation, is that nowhere in Scripture does it say that Christ used *wine* to represent His blood. The only two expressions used are the "cup," or the "fruit of the vine," which suggests it was *unfermented wine*, or grape juice before fermentation. If Christ used *unleavened bread* to represent His body, it follows that He would use *unfermented wine* to represent His blood. Since leaven represented sin, fermentation which partakes of the nature of leaven, also represents sin. Christ is the spotless, sinless, Lamb of God. Both His body and His blood must be represented free from the taint of sin. Hence *unleavened bread and unfermented wine* would be fit, consistent symbols.

Scripture does not indicate the frequency of the celebration of the Lord's Supper—it simply says "for as often as you eat this bread and drink this cup" (1 Corinthians 11:26). The term "often" has to be determined by the believer.

The real significance of the Lord's Supper is that "you proclaim the Lord's death till He comes" (1 Corinthians 11:26). The big question for the believer is, have you appropriated the atoning sacrifice of Christ for your redemption? Christ died to pay the penalty for your sin and mine. Have you repented of your sins and the transgression of the commandments of God? Then Christ's words may be fulfilled to you, "I will not drink henceforth of this fruit of the vine, until that day when I drink it new with you in My Father's kingdom" (Matthew 26:29).

In conclusion, we note that all the foregoing constitutes the Testimony of Jesus, His commands and teachings—and this does not exclude His Sermon on the Mount, or any other teachings. Nevertheless, the Last Day Church—"the rest of her offspring, keep the *commandments of God* and have the *testimony of Jesus Christ*" (Revelation 12:17; Italics supplied). You, dear friend, may belong to the last day church, and be among those "who follow the Lamb wherever He goes" (Revelation 14:4).

Just as the Waldenses and French Huguenots identified themselves with the invisible "Church in the Wilderness," so today there is a visible church that identifies itself with the Last Day Church—"the rest of her offspring." As you apply the identifying marks of the Last Day Church, as outlined with the *commandments of God and the testimony of Jesus*, you will discover the visible representation of that church.

May I conclude with a final thought that arose, when Luther was showing genuine dedication at Wittenberg University. One of the senior professors commented on Luther: "This monk will confuse all the doctors. He will start a new religion and reform the whole Roman Church, for he bases his theology on the writings of the prophets and the apostles. He stands on the Words of Christ, which no philosophy or sophistry can upset or oppose."[3]

Noble reader, may you stand on the "words of Christ"—all the "Testimonies of Jesus," which "no philosophy can oppose."

"Truth is immortal."

EPILOGUE

FINAL APPEAL TO PROTESTANTISM

Protestantism began as a protest against the corruptions of Romanism, and appealed to the Bible as the sole authority in matters of Christian faith and practice. The gist of this book has been an appeal to the Scriptures alone—*sola scriptura* versus the traditions of men. While Luther himself sounded the battle-cry *sola scriptura*, he was defeated on one point by his opponent, the famous debater, Dr. John Eck, who wrote against Luther in 1533:

> There is no mention of the cessation of the Sabbath, and the *institution of Sunday* in the Gospels, or in Paul's writings, or in all the Bible; therefore this has taken place by the apostolic church *instituting it without Scripture*.[1]
>
> *(Italics supplied)*.

It is clear that Luther's *sola scriptura* claim, did not stand up with regard to the institution of Sunday, the day that Protestants observe. Many years later, the 1959 Roman Catholic edition of "The Catechism Simply Explained," after discussing the power of the church in changing the Sabbath to Sunday, browbeat the Protestants with these concluding words:

> Those Christians who believe in the Bible and the Bible only, must have some difficulty in explaining why they keep Sunday holy and not the Sabbath.[2]

I am not able to explain why Luther did not include the Sabbath truth in his reform package, or reject Sunday because it was not based on the Scriptures alone—*sola scriptura*. But, one thing must be noted, and that is, since error had been palmed off by the Great Apostasy for over a thousand years, it would take some time to *restore all the Scriptural truths*. John Robinson, in his farewell address delivered to the Pilgrims, realized this, when he said, "It is not possible the Christian world should come so lately out of such thick antichristian darkness, and that full perfection of knowledge should break forth at once."[3]

Nevertheless, Robinson continued:

> For my part, I cannot sufficiently bewail the condition of the Reformed churches, who are come to a period of religion, and will go at present no farther than the instruments of their reformation. The Lutherans cannot be drawn to go beyond what Luther saw,...and the Calvinists you see, stick fast where they were left by that great man of

> God, who yet saw not all things. This is a misery much to be lamented, for though they were burning and shining lights in their times, yet they penetrated not into the whole counsel of God, but were they now living, would be as willing to embrace further light as that which they first received.[4]

What Robinson described still holds true today, "a misery much to be lamented," when denominations erect creedal barriers, and Christians refuse to accept anything more than what their denomination or creed teaches. Robinson assumed the right attitude when he said:

> If God should reveal anything to you by any *other instrument* of His, be as ready to receive it as ever you were to receive any truth of my ministry, for I am very confident the Lord hath more *truth and light yet to break forth out of His Holy Word.*[5] (Italics supplied)

The situation that prevailed in Christ's day may prevail today, that "light is come into the world, and men loved darkness rather than light" (John 3:19). Paul warns, "For the time will come when they will *not endure sound doctrine*, but according to their own desires, because they have itching ears, they will heap up for themselves teachers; and they will turn their ears away from the *truth*, and be turned aside to *fables*" (2 Timothy 4:3,4; Italics supplied). But, this situation will not prevail for the wise, who are the children of light, who "believe in the light" they have, and continue to "walk while they have the light, lest darkness overtake them" (John 12:35,36). The light of truth is *progressive*, and to those who embrace it, the wise man says, "The path of the just is like the shining sun, that shines ever brighter unto the perfect day" (Proverbs 4:18).

Luther may not have accepted believer's baptism by immersion. But, the Anabaptists and Baptists, another *instrument* of God, brought the truth of adult baptism to the forefront, based on *sola scriptura*. Therefore, those denominations that have not added baptism to their confession of faith, may embrace it now.

Luther did not include the Sabbath of the Lord in his Reformation package (in spite of John Eck's challenge). But, the Sabbatarian Anabaptists and Seventh Day Baptists were God's *instrument* to restore the Sabbath commandment, based on *sola scriptura*. Therefore, Protestantism may add another dimension to their faith, by accepting the Sabbath on the basis of the Protestant principle of *sola scriptura*.

Luther was impressed when he read God's menu for man at Genesis 1, verse 29:

> And God said, 'See, I have given you every herb that yields seed [from Hebrew zera] which is on the face of all the

> earth, and every tree whose fruit yields seed [from Hebrew zera] to you it shall be for food.
>
> *The New King James Version*

Luther extolled the pure vegetarian regimen. Listen to his testimony from his "Lectures on Genesis":

> Nevertheless a diet of herbs rather than of meat would be finer today. Indeed, it is clear that at the beginning of the world herbs served as food and were created for this use, that they might be food for man.[6]

It is interesting to note that the vegetarian diet, comprising grains, fruits, nuts, and vegetables was not just "at the beginning of the world," since Daniel and his companions ordered 'pulse' (from Hebrew zera, at Genesis 1:29), or a vegetarian platter, centuries later (Daniel 1:12).

The point I want to make is this. Although Luther suggested the vegetarian regimen would be *fine* for his day, he never made it part of his Reformation package. And I do not fault him for that. But, here we are, four hundred and fifty years later, with our immense knowledge of the benefits of good nutrition, to present the vegetarian regimen, to become part of our reform package. And it has the support of Scripture, common sense, and scientific research. Isn't that exciting? Go for it!

Enough said, about what Luther did not put into his Reformation package. Considering the gross darkness of his day, Luther accomplished the almost impossible, by shedding light on the greatest truth of all—Salvation by faith alone—*sola fide*. Salvation by faith in the all-sufficient Savior, Jesus Christ. Second, Luther discovered and identified the Antichrist of prophecy. These two discoveries set the tone of the Protestant Reformation. Both were based on sound principles of interpretation: the grammatico-historical exegesis and the historicist method of prophetic interpretation. The strong stance that Luther took on the sole authority of Scripture—*sola scriptura*, set the pace of Protestantism against the traditions of men.

Finish the Reformation

And here we are, four hundred and fifty years after the death of Martin Luther. On this anniversary of his death, I believe the greatest tribute we can pay to Luther is to complete and FINISH THE REFORMATION that he started.

The Reformation can be finished by:

(1) shedding the traditions that Protestantism is still adhering to. Traditions that are not founded on the solid Rock of Protestantism—*sola scriptura*;

(2) shedding the teachings that *run counter* to what Jesus taught in Chapter 9 of this book, thereby constituting a DEPARTURE FROM CHRIST.

The Reformation can be finished by being DRAWN TO CHRIST. The theologian Karl Barth described Count Zinzendorf as a "genuine Christocentric." His life and work have been described in Chapter 8. A genuine Christian is one who is fully committed to Christ, follows Christ, and is obedient to His teachings and commands. The Reformation can be finished by accepting fully the TESTIMONY OF JESUS, as outlined in Chapter 9. It will be completed by obeying Christ's Great Commission: "TO OBSERVE ALL THINGS THAT I HAVE COMMANDED YOU" (Matthew 28:19,20; Capitalization supplied).

"Till we all come to the *unity of the faith* and the knowledge of the Son of God, to a perfect man, to the measure of the stature of the *fullness of Christ*; that we should no longer be children, tossed to and fro and carried about with every wind of doctrine, by the trickery of men, in the cunning craftiness by which they lie in wait to deceive, but speaking the *truth in love*, may grow up in all things into Him who is the *head—Christ*" (Ephesians 4:13–15; Italics supplied).

"For I have not shunned to declare to you the whole counsel of God" (Acts 20:27).

TRUTH IN LOVE—AGAPE

SHALOM!

REFERENCE NOTES

INTRODUCTION

1. Augustine, *On Christian Doctrine*, book 3, chap. 30 in Great Books of the Western World, Number 18, Augustine, (Chicago: Encyclopaedia Britannica, Inc., William Benton, Publisher, 1952).

2. *Ibid.*, *The City of God*, book 20, chap. 12.

3. William M. Landeen, *Martin Luther's Religious Thought* (Mountain View, California: Pacific Press Publishing Assn., 1971), p. 46.

4. William Kelly, ed. *The Collected Writings of J.N. Darby* (London: G. Morrish, n.d.), IV, 31.

CHAPTER 1

1. *Ferraris' Ecclesiastical Dictionary*, (Roman Catholic), article, "Pope" (Rome: Press of the Propaganda, 1899).

2. J.J.I. von Dollinger, *The Pope and the Council* (3 d ed. rev., London: Rivingtons, 1870), p. 91.

3. Augustine, *The City of God*, book 20, chap. 11, 9.

4. *Ibid.*, book 20, chap. 23.

5. Translated from Martin Luther, *Dr. Martin Luther's Sammtliche Schriften*, ed. J.G. Walch (St. Louis: Concordia Publishing House, 1881–1910), VI, cols. 898–900.

6. J.H. Merle d'Aubigne, *History of the Reformation of the Sixteenth Century* (New York: Worthington Co., n.d.), book 6, chap. 3.

CHAPTER 2

1. In the year 1689, Drue Cressener D.D., later Junior Proctor of the University of Cambridge, was the first to date the rise of the little horn from the Justinian era, concluding the 1,260 years dominance about 1800. See Cressener, *The Judgments of God upon the Roman Catholick Church* p. 309.

2. H.G. Wells, *Outline of History* (1920) p. 526.

3. H. Grattan Guinness, *Romanism and the Reformation, From the Standpoint of Prophecy* (New York: A.C. Armstrong & Son, 1887), pp. 41–43.

Here Guinness outlines the main points to identify the "little horn": location; time of origin; the nature—different; moral character—pompous words; the lawlessness—intention to change times and laws; opposition to saints; the duration—1,260 years; the doom. These eight points "do all meet in the Roman Papacy," says Guinness.

4. Translated from Andreas Osiander, *Vermutung von den letzten Zeiten und dem Ende der Welt, aus der heiligen Schrifftgezogen* (Nurnberg: J. Petreius, 1545), chap. 4.

5. *Ibid.*

6. *Ibid.*

7. C. Graham Botha, and C. Struik, *The French Refugees at the Cape* (3 d ed.; Cape Town: Pty. Ltd., 1970), p. 30.

8. J.A. Wylie, *The History of Protestantism* (3 vols.; London: Cassell & Co. Ltd., n.d.), book 22, chap. 7.

9. *A Historic Sketch of the Huguenot Church, Charleston, South Carolina* (The News & Courier Book Presses, 1886), p. 6.

CHAPTER 3

1. Codex Justinianus, lib. 3, tit.12,3 translated in Philip Schaff, D.D., *History of the Christian Church* (seven-volume edition, New York: Charles Scribner's Sons, 1902), III, 380.

2. Charles Joseph Hefele, *A History of the Christian Councils*, trans. H.N. Oxenham (Edinburgh: T. and T. Clark, 1896), II, 316.

3. Eusebius, *Life of Constantine*, book 4, chap. 24, translated in Nicene & Post-Nicene Fathers, (2 d series; New York) vol. I.

4. *Ibid.*, Book 3, chap. 15.

5. Ernest F. Henderson, trans. & ed. *Select Historical Documents of the Middle Ages* (London: George Bell & Sons, 1903), pp. 319–329.

6. Dollinger, *The Pope and the Council*, p. 105.

7. David S. Schaff, *The Middle Ages* (New York: Charles Scribner's Sons 1907–1910), 1 vol. in 2 (Philip Schaff, *History of the Christian Church*, vol. 5, parts 1 & 2) part 2, pp. 25–28.

8. *Ibid.*

9. Augustine, *The City of God*, book 20, chap. 19.

10. *Ibid.*

11. Translated from Jerome, Epistle 121 (to Algasia), in J.P. Migne, *Patrologiae Cursus completus,...Series Latina* (Parisiis: Apud J.P. Migne, 1841–1846) XXII, col. 1037.

12. Translated from Joachim, *Liber Concordie Novi ac Veteris Testamenti* (Book of the Harmony of the New and Old Testament) (Venetijs: Per Simonem de Luere, 1519), fol. 95 r,v.

13. *Ibid.*, fol. 12v.

14. Translated from Johannes Turmair, *Annalium Boiorum Libri Septem* (Bavarian Annals), Ioanne Aventino [pseud.] Autore (Ingoldstadt: Per Alexandrum und Samuelem Weissenhorn, 1554), p. 684.

CHAPTER 4

1. J.A. Wylie, *History of the Waldenses* (Mountain View California: Pacific Press Publishing Assn., 1977), pp. 10,11.

2. Translated from the report of Peter the Inquisitor in Döllinger, *Beitrage zur Sektengeschichte des Mittelalters* (Munchen: C.H. Beck'sche Verlagsbuchhandlung, 1890),II, 306, sec. 3.

3. Henri Arnoud, *The Glorious Recovery by the Vaudois of Their Valleys*, trans. and ed, H.D. Acland, (London: John Murray, 1827), p. xiv.

4. *Ibid.*, p. xiii.

5. Translated from Morel, letter to Oecolampadius, in A.W. Dieckhoff, *Die Waldenser in Mittelalter* (Gottingen: Bei Vandenhoeck und Ruprecht, 1851) p. 368.

6. Samuel Morland, *The History of the Evangelical Churches of the Valleys of Piemont* (London: Printed by H. Hills for A. Byfield, 1658), p. 14.

7. *Ibid.*, p. 113.

8. *Bible Vaudoise*, public library of Lyons, No. 60.

9. Alexis Muston, D.D., *The Israel of the Alps* (Glasgow: W.G. Blackie & Co., Printers, 1857), I 20,21.

10. Dollinger, *Beitrage* II, 327, 662.

11. A. Monastier, *A History of the Vaudois Church* (rev.; New York: Lane & Scott, 1849), p. 104.

12. Walter Map, Walter Map's "*De Nugis Curialium,*" trans. M.R. James (London: The Honourable Society of Cymmrodorian, 1923). pp. 65, 66.

13. *Ibid.*

14. Translated from Burchard of Ursperg, *Burchardi et Cuonradi Urspergensium Chronicon*, in *Monumenta Germaniae Historica, Scriptores* (Hannoverae: Impensis Bibliopolii Hahniani, 1826–1913), XXIII, 376.

15. Monastier, p. 37; as quoted by Dr. William S. Gilly.

16. *Ibid.*, p. 38; as quoted by Dr. William S. Gilly.

17. *Ibid.*, pp. 65–67.

18. James H. Todd D.D., *The Books of the Vaudois* (Dublin: Hodges Smith & Co., 1865), pp. 126,132.

19. Monastier, p. 103.

20. Muston, pp. 15,16.

21. Giorgio Tourn, *The Waldensians, The First 800 Years (1174–1974)*, trans. C.P. Merlino (Turin: Claudiana Editrice, 1980) pp. 36–38. Distributed by Friendship Press N.Y.—N.Y. 10115.

22. *Ibid.*, p. 36.

23. The entire Treatise On Antichrist is recorded in Morland, *The History of the Evangelical Churches of the Valleys of Piemont*, pp. 142–159.

24. Translated from [Passau Inquisitor], *Reineri Ordinis Praedicatorum Contra Waldenses Haereticos, Liber*, ed. J. Gretser, in *Maxima Bibliotheca Veterum Patrum, et Antiquorum Scriptorum Ecclesiasticorum*, ed. M. de la Bigne (Lugduni: Apud Anissonius, 1677), XXV, 265.

25. "Noble Lesson" recorded in Morland, p. 118.

26. Monastier, pp. 81,82.

27. This summary from the *Treatise On Antichrist* has caught the attention of many, such as Elliott, *Horae*, II, 397; Guinness, *History Unveiling Prophecy*, p. 91.

28. Wylie, *History of the Waldenses*, pp. 50,51.

29. Botha, p. 10.

CHAPTER 5

1. Edward Bishop Elliott, *Horae Apocalypticae*; or, *A Commentary on the Apocalypse* (4 vols. 5th ed., London: Seeley, Jackson, and Halliday, 1862), II, 394.

2. John Wyclif, *The English Works of Wyclif Hitherto Unprinted*, ed. F.D. Matthew (London: Published for the Early English Text Society, by Trubner & Co., 1880) pp. 458 FF.

3. Translated from Luther's preface in John Purvey, *Commentarius in Apocalypsin Ante Centum Annos Editus* (Vittembergae: [n.n.], 1528).

4. E.H. Gillett, *The Life and Times of John Huss or the Bohemian Reformation of the Fifteenth Century* (Boston: Gould & Lincoln, 1863), II, 570.

5. Elliott, II, 450.

6. Translated from J.D. Mansi, ed. *Sacrorum conciliorum nova, et amplissima collectio* (Parisiis: Huberto Welter, 1901–1927) XXXII, ed. 761.

7. Translated from Mansi, XXXII, col. 803.

8. Elliott, II, 89,101; Guinness, *History Unveiling Prophecy*, p. 119.

9. J.H. Merle d'Aubigne, *History of the Reformation of the Sixteeth Century* (5 vols.; New York: Worthington Co., n.d.) I, 130.

10. *Ibid.*, I, 165.

11. *Ibid.*, I, 170.

12. *Ibid.*, I. 203.

13. *Ibid.*, I. 201.

14. *Ibid.*, II, 13.

15. Translated from Luther *Schriften*, XV, col. 1639.

16. Philip Schaff, *History of the Christian Church* vol. 5, parts 1 and 2 written by his son David S. Schaff, (New York: Charles Scribner's Sons, 1882–1910), VI, 248.

17. H. Grattan Guinness, D.D., *History Unveiling Prophecy or Time as an Interpreter* (New York: Fleming H. Revell Coy., 1905), p. 121.

18. *Ibid.*, pp. 126,127. The footnote lists the works of Luther, Knox, Tyndale, Latimer, Hooper, Ridley, Cranmer, Jewel, Coverdale, Foxe, Fulke, Grindal, Bale, Bradford, Beacon, Bullinger, Rogers, Sandys, Norden, Nowell, Hutchinson, Whittaker, Whitgift, Melanchthon, Zwingli, Calvin.

19. Philip Schaff, *The Creeds of Christendom, With a History and Critical Notes* (New York: Harper & Brothers, 1919), III, 658, 659, chap. 25. sec. 6; and pp. 672,783, chap. 33, sec. 3.

CHAPTER 6

1. B.J. Kidd, D.D., *The Counter-Reformation, 1550–1600* (London: Society for Promoting Christian Knowledge, 1933), pp. 59,60.

2. *Ibid.*, pp. 64–66.

3. Joseph Tanner, *Daniel and the Revelation: The Chart of Prophecy and our place in it. A Study of the Historical & Futurist Interpretation* (London: Hodder & Stoughton, 1898), pp. 16,17.

4. Elliott, IV, 480–483.

5. Drue Cressener, *The Judgments of God Upon the Roman Catholick Church* (London: Printed for Richard Chiswell, 1689), p. 312.

6. Elliott, IV, pp. 554,555.

7. Guinness, *History Unveiling Prophecy*, p. 289.

8. *Ibid.*, p. 288.

9. *Ibid.*, p. 287,288.

10. *Ibid.*, p. 290.

11. *Ibid.*, p. 284.

12. Tanner, p. 17.

CHAPTER 7

1. K.S. Latourette, *A History of Christianity* (London: Eyre & Spottiswoode, n.d.) p. 786.

2. Henry S. Burrage, *A History of the Anabaptists in Switzerland* (New York: Burt Franklin Published by Lennox Hill Pub., 1973), pp.

104,105,108,119. I am indebted to this author for much of the story of Anabaptism.

3. Quoted in Peter De Rosa, *Vicars of Christ, The Dark Side of the Papacy* (New York: Crown Publishers, Inc., 1988) p. 178.

4. Quoted in J.N. Andrews, *History of the Sabbath and First Day of the Week* (2nd ed.; Battle Creek, Michigan, 1873), p. 639.

5. *Ibid.*, pp. 640,641.

6. *Ibid.*, pp. 641–649; *Andrews University Studies* 6 (January 1968) pp. 23–27; Ministry, (January 1987) pp. 15–17.

7. Quoted in J.N. Andrews, pp. 729, 730.

8. Le Roy E. Froom, *The Prophetic Faith of Our Fathers, The Historical Development of Prophetic Interpretation* (4 vols.; Washington, D.C.: Review & Herald Publishing Assn., 1946–1954), IV, 906–919.

9. *Ibid.*, IV 917.

CHAPTER 8

1. Quoted in J.N. Andrews pp. 754–756.

2. Guinness, *History Unveiling Prophecy*, p. 167.

3. John Wesley, *Forty Four Sermons, Sermons On Several Occasions* (London: The Epworth Press, 1961), pp. 252,253.

4. *Ibid.*, pp. 386–393.

5. *Ibid.*, pp. 255,391,393.

6. John Wesley, *Explanatory Notes Upon the New Testament* (vol. 3; lst American ed.; Philadelphia: Pritchard & Hall, 1791), pp. 290–296, v.1–5; 299, v.ii.

CHAPTER 9

1. *Peake's Commentary*, Comments on Matthew 24.

2. Michael Geddes, *Church History of Ethiopia*, p. 88.

3. Edith Simon, *The Reformation, Great Ages of Man* (New York: Silver Burdett Co., 1966), p. 20.

EPILOGUE

1. John Eck, *Enchiridion Locorum Communium adversus Lutheranos* (Handbook of Commonplaces against the Lutherans) 1533, pp. 78,79. English quotation in Frank H. Yost, Ph.D. *The Early Christian Sabbath* (Mountain View, California: Pacific Press Publishing Assn., 1947), p. 70.

2. Canon Cafferata, *The Catechism Simply Explained* (London: Burns Oates & Washbourne Ltd. 1959), p. 84.

3. W. Carlos Martyn, *The Pilgrim Fathers of New England* (1867), pp. 70,71.

4. Daniel Neal, *History of the Puritans* (1848), I, 269,270.

5. Martyn, p. 7.

6. Martin Luther, "Lectures on Genesis," *Luther's Works*, (St. Louis: Concordia Publishing House, 1958) I, 36.

APPENDICES

APPENDIX A

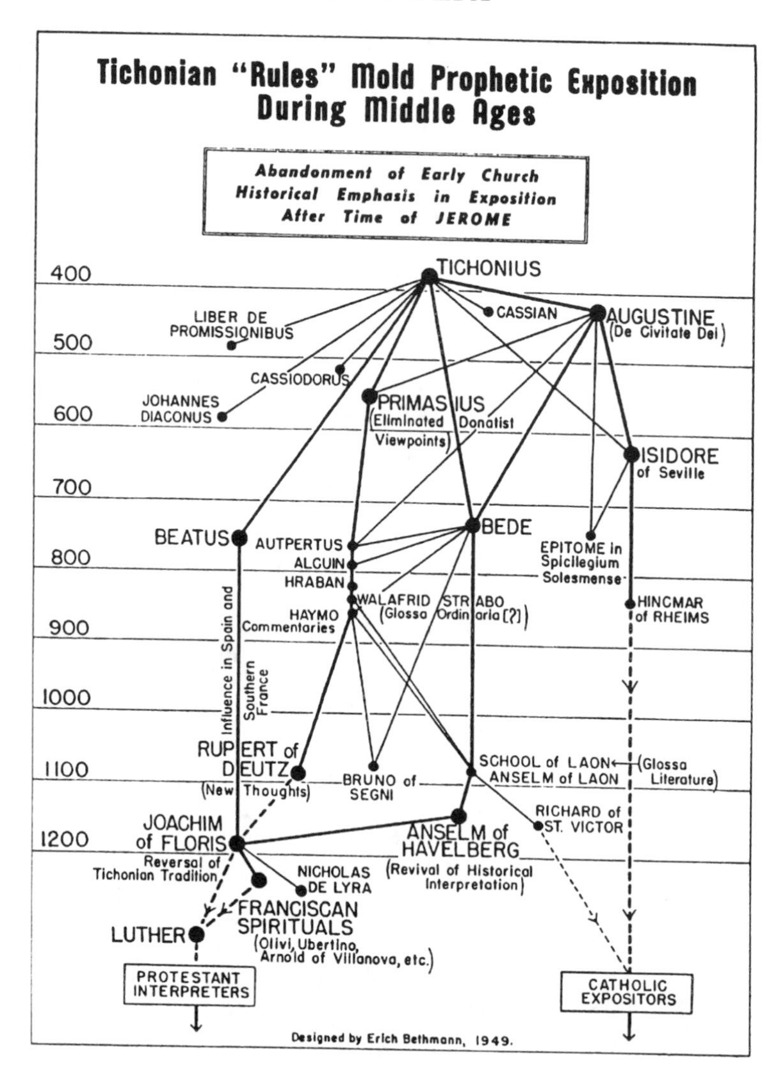

Graph—L.E. Froom, I, 545

Chart of the Tichonian Influence for Seven Centuries
Tichonius and his Seven Rules of Interpretation had a molding influence for seven centuries. He introduced a purely Mystical, or Spiritual exegesis of the Apocalypse (Revelation), eliminating application to Material Historical events. 700 years after Tichonius, Joachim of Floris and his followers, reinstated the Historical Interpretation of the Symbols of the Apocalypse to become the original Protestant position.

APPENDIX B

Chart E.B. Elliott, IV, 421

JOACHIM ABBAS' APOCALYPTIC SCHEME.

A.D.	1—100.	100—310.	310—550.	550—800.	800—1200.	1200—1260	1260. . . .
SEALS.	I. Christ and Apostolic Church triumphing over Judaism.	II. Roman Pagan Persecutions and Blood-shedding.	III. Arians, with false balance and Scripture perversion.	IV. Mahomet and the Saracens' desolations.	V. Persecutions and Martyrdoms by Saracens in Spain and Mauritania.	VI. Babylon's judgment day begins. Christianity visibly supprest. Antichrist's 4 evil Angels. Sealing Vision.	VII. Half-hour's silence, the *Sabbath.* Perhaps the last half of the 3½ times.
TRUMPETS.	I. Judaizers' indurated as hail. ⅓ of Christianized Jews apostatize.	II. Nicolaitans' burning mountain, in the sea of Gentilism.	III. Arius' falling star.	Woe denouncing Gregory. IV. Light of Monks and Virgins quenched by the Saracens.	V. Locusts, or Pathareni.	VI. Confederacy of Saracens, Turks, Moors, and Northern Germans against Rome.—Mystery of iniquity preparing.	Mystery ended. Antichrist extinguished. VII. Sabbath beginning, as in Apoc. xx.
VIALS.	I. on Jews & Judaizers.	II. on Gentilizing recreants.	III. on Arian Bishops and Doctors.	IV. on vain and hypocritical Monastics.	V. on Monastics apostatizing to the Beast.	VI. Euphrates of Roman power dried up—Antichrist's 3 frogs.	VII. Air purified for Church's bridal
WITNESSES AND TRAVAILING WOMAN.	The The Holy	42 months or 1260 days in the sense of City of Christendom	1260 days of the 42 generations, *partially* Gentile-trod	Christ's gen Woman in or 1260 —Greek Church ejected	eral Witnessing the Wilderness years. and given to Enoch. Apoc.	Body. Moses, Elias. 3½ yrs. Gentiles.	rit. End: to God.
BEAST'S SEVEN AND EIGHT HEADS.	I. Antichristian Jews, under Herod. (=Daniel's 1st Beast.)	II. Roman Pagans, Nero to Diocletian. (= Daniel's 2nd Beast.)	III. IV. & V. Arian Greeks, Goths, and Vandals. (= Daniel's 3rd four-	VI. Arian Lombards. headed Beast.)	VII. Mahometan, Saracen, or Turkish Empire; now under Saladin. (= Daniel's 4th Beast.)	VIII. The 7th Head wounded, revives as Daniel's Little Horn; still under Saladin.	of the Spi of the end known only
SEVEN CHIEF KINGS.	I. Herod. II. Nero.		III. Constantius.	IV. Mahomet.	V. German Ghibelline Emperors. VI. "He who is;" Saladin A.D. 1195.	VII. Saladin over the decem-regal anti-Romish confederacy. Antichrist.	Age Time When to

Apocalyptic Scheme of Joachim of Floris

Notice 7 Seals, 7 Trumpets, 2 Witnesses, and the Sun-clothed woman of Revelation 6 to 8, 11, 12, commence in the First Century and run simultaneously through Historic Time, to the "Time of the End," from A.D. 1260; according to Joachim's view in his day and age.

APPENDIX C

GRAMMATICO-HISTORICAL EXEGESIS

Grammatico-historical exegesis describes the simplest, straight forward, method of Bible Study employed since the time of the Protestant Reformation. It includes the following principles.

(1) *Lexical.* This means the normal, grammatical meaning and usage of the words at the time of writing, ascertaining the common sense meaning.

(2) *Syntactic.* This means to understand the grammatical construction and principles pertaining to the time of writing, in the languages of the Old Testament, or the New Testament.

(3) *Contextual.* This means one must consider what was written before, and what was written after, the passage of Scripture under study. The entire trend of thought must be explored.

(4) *Historical.* This means one ascertains the historical circumstances, the background, the time, and place that brought about the writing under investigation. The culture, customs, and manners of the people are also taken into account.

(5) *According to the Analogy of Scripture.* While there is an underlying unity of theme running through the Scriptures, it is incumbent upon the reader to compare Scripture with Scripture. The study of a passage of Scripture demands the gathering, marshaling, and comparing of other passages, that bear upon that given subject.

Grammatico-historical exegesis certainly gives attention to the literal meaning of a passage of Scripture. But it does recognize metaphorical, symbolic, figurative, and poetic expressions of language. It is easy to see that the apocalyptic prophecies of Daniel and Revelation employ metaphor and symbol. But these are generally interpreted within the context, without leaving it to the imagination to run wild.

BIBLIOGRAPHY

SELECT BIBLIOGRAPHY

Prımary and Secondary Sources listed in Reference Notes will not be repeated in this Bibliography, except for a few Select Secondary Source Books.

Bainton, Roland H. *Here I Stand A Life of Martin Luther.* Nashville, Tennessee: Abingdon Press, 1956.

Boyd, Jesse L. *A History of Baptists in America Prior to 1845.* New York; The American Press, 1957.

Brackney, William H. *The Baptists.* New York: Greenwood Press, 1988.

Burrage, Henry S. *A History of the Anabaptists in Switzerland.* New York: Burt Franklin, Published by Lenox Hill Pub., 1973.

Comba, Emilio. D.D. *History of the Waldenses of Italy From Their Origin to the Reformation.* Trans. Teofilo E. Comba. London: Truslove & Shirley, 1889.

d'Aubigne, J.H. Merle. *History of the Reformation of the Sixteenth Century.* New York: Worthington Co., n.d.

De Rosa, Peter. *Vicars of Christ The Dark Side of the Papacy.* New York: Crown Publishers, Inc., 1988.

Dollinger, J.J.I. von. *The Pope and the Council.* 3 d ed., rev. London: Rivingtons, 1870.
This book was put on the Index of Prohibited Books just before Vatican I, because it challenged papal claims to infallibility. Professor Dollinger was later excommunicated and stripped of his position.

Elliott, Edward B. *Horae Apocalypticae*; or, *A Commentary on the Apocalypse.* 4 vols. 5th ed. London: Seeley, Jackson, & Halliday, 1862.
Appendix 1 in vol. IV has a 288 page History of Apocalyptic Interpretation of value.
Elliott's work covers the rise and spread of two Jesuit systems of prophetic interpretation.

Froom, Le Roy E. *The Prophetic Faith of Our Fathers The Historical Development of Prophetic Interpretation.* 4 vols. Washington, D.C.: Review & Herald Publishing Assn., 1946–1954.
Besides the Prophetic element, Froom's monumental work is a valuable resource on the history of the Christian Church.
Abundant original source material is accurately documented.

Gilly, William S. D.D. *Waldensian Researches.*
London: C.J.G. & F. Rivington, 1831.

Guinness, H. Grattan. D.D. *History Unveiling Prophecy, or Time as an Interpreter.*
New York: Fleming H. Revell Co., 1905.

Hamilton, J.T. *A History of the Church known as the Moravian Church.*
Bethlehem, Pennsylvania: Times Publishing Co., 1900.

Kidd, B.J. D.D. *The Counter-Reformation 1500–1600.*
London: Society for Promoting Christian Knowledge, 1933.

Landeen, William M. *Martin Luther's Religious Thought.*
Mountain View, California: Pacific Press Publishing Assn., 1971.

Latourette, K.S. *A History of Christianity.*
London: Eyre & Spottiswoode, n.d.

Liechty, Daniel. *Andreas Fischer and the Sabbatarian Anabaptists, An Early Reformation Episode in East Central Europe.*
Scottsdale, Pennsylvania: Herald Press, 1988.

Lindsay, T.M. D.D. *The Reformation.*
Edinburgh: T. & T. Clark, 1956.

Mitchell, A.W. *The Waldenses: Sketches of the Evangelical Christians of the Valleys of Piedmont.*
Philadelphia: Presbyterian Board of Publication, 1853.

Monastier, A. *A History of the Vaudois Church.* Rev.
New York: Lane & Scott, 1849.

Morland, Samuel. *The History of the Evangelical Churches of the Valleys of Piemont.*
London: Printed by H. Hills for A. Byfield, 1658.

Muston, Alexis. D.D. *The Israel of the Alps.* 2 vols.
Glasgow: W.G. Blackie & Co. Printers, 1857.
This work contains a useful exhaustive Bibliography (92 pages) with Bibliographic Essay. The work makes a strong case for the Origin of the Vaudois (Italian Waldenses), anterior to Peter Waldo. When Muston published his first "*History of the Vaudois*" in 1834, he was banished from his land. His book was put on the Index of Prohibited Books, together with the reprinted works of other earlier Vaudois natives, Gilles and Leger. Pope Paul VI discontinued the Index in 1966.

Rican, Rudolf. *The History of the Unity of Brethren, A Protestant Hussite Church in Bohemia and Moravia.* Trans. C.D. Crews.
Bethlehem, Pennsylvania: Dept. of Publications & Communications, Moravian Church, 1992.

Sanford, Don A. *A Choosing People: The History of Seventh Day Baptists.*
Nashville, Tennessee: Broadman Press, 1992.

Sanford, Don A. *Newport History.* Bulletin of the Newport Historical Society, vol. LXVI, Part 1, Number 226.
Portsmouth, Rhode Island: Hamilton Printing Co., 1994.

Tanner, Joseph. *Daniel and the Revelation: The Chart of Prophecy and our place in it, A Study of the Historical and Futurist Interpretation.*
London: Hodder & Stoughton, 1898.

Todd, James H. D.D. *The Books of the Vaudois.*
Dublin: Hodges Smith & Co., 1865.

Tourn, Giorgio. *The Waldensians The First 800 Years (1174–1974).*
Trans. C.P. Merlino.
Turin: Claudiana Editrice, 1980.

Wakefield, Walter L. *Heresy, Crusade and the Inquisition in Southern France 1100–1250.*
Berkely: University of California Press, 1974.

Walsh, Mary E. *The Wine of Roman Babylon.*
Nashville, Tennessee: The Southern Publishing Assn., 1968.

Wylie, J.A. *The History of Protestantism.* 3 vols.
London: Cassell & Co. Ltd., n.d.

Other books by TEACH Services, Inc.

1844 Vol. 1–3 *Jerome L. Clark* $29.95
These volumes go forth in the hope that it will give the reader a deeper insight into the atmosphere of reform which permeated the time in which arose the Millerite Movement, the seedbed of the Seventh-day Adventist Church. Such an atmosphere made people receptive to change and provided the attitude of mind which made the widespread dissemination of new ideas possible. Surely it was in the providence of God that the "great Second Advent Movement" arose at such a time.

The Antichrist 666 *William Josiah Sutton* . . . . $ 8.95
Positive proof for Bible Believing People: Who the beast is; Who his image is; What the mark of the beast is; How to count the number of the beast. Edited by Roy Allan Anderson, D.D.

The Anti-Christ Exposed *Dan Jarrard* . . . . $ 5.95
A biblical and historical study of the counterfeit religious system which is against God and His people.

The Celtic Church in Britain *Leslie Hardinge* . . . . $ 8.95
This is an authoritative study of the beliefs and practice of the Celtic Church which at the same time holds much interest for the non-specialist, containing as it does fascinating descriptions of the life of the early Celtic Christians in their monastic walled villages modelled on the Old Testament cities of refuge. Their elaborate penitential discipline was based on Old Testament compensatory regulations. Obedience to the Scriptures led them to establish a remarkable theocracy based on the laws of the Pentateuch and including the keeping of the Seventh-day Sabbath.

Children's Bible Lessons *Bessie White* . . . . $ 3.95
These seven Children's Bible Lessons are prepared for use during Evangelistic Meetings, Bible seminars, Vacation Bible Schools, or at the Church's discretion.

Christian Faith & Religious Freedom *Olsen, V.N.* . . . . $ 8.95
The theological grounding provided in this book is an important antidote to the tendency of many to base their arguments on religious freedom and church/state issues on political or constitutional grounds. Dr. Olsen makes an important contribution to our thinking by making us face the theological bedrock of any Christian approach to these topics.

Convert's Catechism *Peter Geiermann* . . . . $ 2.50
The quoted statement on changing solemnity from Saturday to Sunday can be found in this reproduction.

Divine Philosophy & Science of Health & Healing *Paulien* $19.95
All of the principles of the Bible and the Spirit of Prophecy are designed to allow us to function in perfect harmony with God Himself. This book discusses the methods and means of healthful living. It deals with going back to First Things, and relying by faith upon the substances which God has established for our benefit.

Dove of Gold *Leslie Hardinge* . . . . $ 7.95
This book approaches the vast subject of the Holy Spirit viewing His functions through illustrations He himself has selected as vehicles for the revelation of His character and work. As one observes the related aspects of the nature and function of the natural object used as a symbol, the work of the Holy Spirit will become clearer, and His disposition of concern and affection much more appealing.

Earthly Life of Jesus *Ken LeBrun* $19.95
Biblical accounts of each event in Christ's earthly life carefully arranged together from the KJV Bible. Words of Jesus in red with full index.

Fire Bell in the Night *Ralph Moss* . . . . $ 5.95
News items and stories from both the secular press and from religious newspapers, along with journals and articles by secular and religious authors will be linked with Bible prophecy to reveal a most startling scenario in just the last few years, and to lay a case to expose an undreamed of enemy who is rapidly winning the confidence of most of this world's inhabitants.

From Eden to Eden *J. H. Waggoner* . . . . $ 9.95
A most interesting study of the more important historic and prophetic portions of the Scriptures.

God's Justice—Administered in Love *Dick Beman* . . . . $ 5.95
You can learn the secret of how to stand firm in the Judgment, without being afraid, and yet maintain a healthy, respectful fear of God.

Gospel In Creation *E. J. Waggoner* . . . . $ 6.95
This book directs our wandering gaze to the open pages of God's created works as the expression of the gospel, the power of God to save from sin. Facsimile Reprint.

Helps to Bible Study *J. L. Shuler* . . . . $ 2.95
A Bible marking system which contains Bible studies covering twenty-eight topics including "The Second Coming," "The Seal of the Living God," "Bible Temperance," and "Christian in Dress." It is simple and practical in its approach, and will benefit all ages.

Holy Spirit Seminar *Harold Penninger*........................ $ 7.95
A collection of Holy Spirit Seminars for study, inspiration, etc.

Hydrotherapy—Simple Treatments *Thomas/Dail* .... $ 8.95
Help your body overcome common diseases using hydrotherapy and simple home treatments.

The Illuminati 666 *William Josiah Sutton* .... $ 8.95
Find out about the Illuminati, its startling history, and how powerful it has become. Includes a study of the origins of false religions, and the forms they are taking today. Introduction by Roy Allan Anderson, D.D.

The Justified Walk *Frank Phillips*.......................... $ 8.95
Before you can rightly tackle a problem, you must first be able to clearly understand its nature. Before you can discuss it with others, you must first define your terms. In this book Elder Phillips makes clear how the plan of salvation works in our daily lives. Faith, Grace, Sin, Justification, Sanctification and Righteousness are made real and tangible.

Lessons On Faith *Jones & Waggoner* .... $ 6.95
This is a compilation of articles and sermons given in the 1890's by Jones and Waggoner on Righteousness By Faith.

Let the Holy Spirit Speak *Garrie Fraser Williams*............. $ 4.95
A remarkable new book that is not just a study guide but a unique resource of Bible study methods and small group information.

Letters to the Churches *M. L. Andreasen* .... $ 7.95
A collection of letters objecting to statements in the book *SDA's Answer to Questions on Doctrine*. Andreasen was Conference President, President of Union College, and Secretary at the General Conference.

Living the Life of Enoch *E. G. White* .... $ 7.95
We are to live the Enoch life! This is our commission. and this is a twofold work—to develop a character of righteousness by living a life of personal purity and pleading with God; to teach a lesson of godliness by kindly acts and warning and pleading with men.

Living Fountains or Broken Cisterns *E. A. Sutherland*......... $12.95
This book tells how we should set up our education systems to follow the heavenly blueprint. The goal is to have the best Christian schools in the world.

Mystical Medicine *Warren Peters* . . . . $ 7.95
Many people today have come to believe that our modern, technological system of health care in the Western world isn't proving to be the great boon that it was once thought to be. Frustrated and disillusioned people are turning to "more natural" methods of treatment. As we become aware of the intimate connection between the physical, mental and spiritual aspects of our nature, we are flocking to holistic medicine by the thousands.

National Sunday Law *A. T. Jones* . . . . $ 7.95
This book is a report of an argument made concerning the national Sunday bill that was introduced by Senator Blair in the fiftieth Congress.

Pioneer Stories *Arthur W. Spalding* . . . . $ 9.95
It is good for children to know what their fathers and mothers did; for sometimes that makes a pattern of what the children should do. Especially is this true if the children are set to finish the work their parents began. And that is the reason why this book is written, to tell the children of the pioneers in the second advent movement the beginnings of that movement, and reasons why they are to carry it on.

Power of Prayer *E. G. White*. . . . . $ 7.95
Prayer is our connection with God—our strength, our bridge to heaven! As we pray, the Holy Spirit Himself unites in our petitions and "maketh intercession for us." We are not alone in our battle of life; all heaven is on our side!

Principles To Live By *Mel Rees* . . . . $ 4.95
Dominion calls for individual decision and action—therefore, God gave man guiding principles to live by.

Rome's Challenge *Catholic Mirror* . . . . $ .99
"The pages of this brochure unfold to the reader one of the most glaringly conceivable contradictions existing between the practice and theory of the Protestant world, and unsusceptible of any rational solution, the theory claiming the Bible alone as the teacher.

The Sabbath *M. L. Andreasen*. . . . . $ 9.95
Attacks upon the Sabbath throughout the ages have been numerous and persistent, and they have all been grounded upon human reasoning as as against the command of God. Men can see no reason why any other day than one commanded by God is not just as good. Men cannot see why one day in seven is not just as good as the seventh day. The answer, of course, is that the difference lies in God's command. It is at this point that man's reason sets aside a positive command of God. It is not merely a question of this or that day, but the greater question of obedience to God's command.

Shadows of His Sacrifice *Leslie Hardinge* .... $ 7.95
Understanding Jesus through the types and symbols of the Sanctuary. God has given us the details of the sanctuary so we can study each part minutely. Only then will we be able to see Christ in His fullness. Jesus is the Sacrifice. He is also the priest. He is the Shekinah, and He is also the veil. He is "every whit!"

Story of Daniel the Prophet *S. N. Haskell*.................... $11.95
This book especially applicable to our day: points out the immediate future and in its simplicity will attract many who might not be inclined to read deep, argumentative works. Facsimile Reprint.

Story of the Seer of Patmos *S. N. Haskell*.................... $12.95
The Book of Revelation pronounces a blessing upon everyone who reads it or hears it. Facsimile Reprint.

Studies in Daniel and Revelation *Kraid Ashbaugh* .... $ 4.95
A convenient handbook containing paraphrases of EG White's comments after each verse in the books of Daniel & Revelation.

Studies in the Book of Hebrews *E. J. Waggoner* .... $ 6.95
A series of studies given at the General Conference of 1897. The Bible studies that Elder Waggoner gave each day, are presented as live and full of hope for each Bible student today.

Subtle Challenge to God's Authority *Milton Crane* .... $ 5.50
Satan's deceptions are many and subtle. He has concentrated his attack on God's authority.

Such A Cloud of Witnesses *Milton Crane*.................... $ 4.95
You are called to be a witness for or against the government of God. Will your testimony help God or aid His enemy?

Truth Triumphant *B. G. Wilkinson*......................... $12.95
The history of God's true Church from Ireland, to the Waldenses, the struggle to preserve the Bible and the pure doctrine of the apostles is disclosed. Facsimile Reprint.

Victory and Self-Mastery *J. N. Tindall*..................... $ 5.95
How Christ maintained a sinless character in a fallen, sinful, human nature. Facsimile Reprint.

Walking With God *Harold Penninger*......................... $ 7.95
God's plan provided that man could learn how to walk with Him as Enoch did before he was translated. This book gives the experiences of some of the people of the Bible who have followed in His footsteps such as Abraham, Enoch, Job, Elijah, Daniel, Peter, John and Paul.

The Word Was Made Flesh *Ralph Larson* . . . . $ 8.95
This book is on the human nature of Christ, with a limited, rather specialized objective. Dr. Larson does not deal directly with the whole issue of Christ's human nature. He traces the understanding of this aspect of Christology within the Seventh-day Adventist church from 1852–1952, providing a fairly comprehensive survey of historical data.